A VOICE IN THE WILDERNESS

Finding God in Confusion

by Annie K Heathcoat

First published in Great Britain 2019

PipTil Publishing
Glen Garth
Wheatley Rd
Halifax
HX3 5AA

Printed and bound by BookPrinting UK, Peterborough, UK

ISBN: 978-1-9164031-4-7

For the many unnamed angels who help us to hear the voice of God amidst the shrieks of the wild beasts.

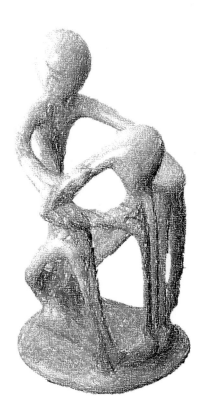

Copyright Information

Contents

About the Illustrations

The illustrations in this collection are all the work of the author. Some of the photographs on which they are based were taken specifically for this project, whilst others have been drawn from an extensive collection taken over a period of thirty years. The ways in which they are presented is a departure from previous work because many of them have been manipulated with computer programmes[1] to reduce background distraction, or to create deliberate artistic effect. They are included to give context, enhance the text, or provide a focus for reflection. High resolution, colour, digital copies of the images are available on the website www.piptil.co.uk for personal use or for projection in public worship.

Details of the subjects and locations of the photographs are given at the end of the book to avoid interrupting the flow of the text with captions.

---

[1] *Adobe Photoshop Express for Android* and *Sketch Camera for Android*

The *Voice in the Wilderness* Project
Finding God in Confusion

This work is a collection of meditations on the events of Holy Week from the perspective of those who walked alongside Jesus and shared his agony. Although there is a focus on mental health, this does not mean that these meditations are only relevant to those who have been affected by such issues, they can be relevant to people going through difficult times that are not related to mental health, and who need to know that God is beside them in their confusion and pain too. The meditations can also stand alone as reflections on the last week of Jesus' earthly life and could be used as such in public worship, or as part of a discussion group.

This work is not a self-help book demonstrating how faith can heal mental health issues, or a handbook on how to handle difficult or painful episodes of mental illness in which we find ourselves caught up. I have no expertise to offer the latter, only my own experiences on which to draw. For the former, I am extremely wary of any implication that lack of faith or the inability to hear the voice of God impedes recovery, as this is not what a loving, faithful God would say. Faith strengthens and upholds us through mental health and other painful episodes, and that in itself may lead to healing, but faith on its own is not a magic cure or a panacea for all ills. It is a tool we may use, alongside medical expertise and talking therapies, which are also God-given gifts. There are times when I have been so confused that I have "ridden the wings of faith" of others, by which I mean I have allowed them to believe for me and pray for me when I could not. Indeed, the origins of this book lie in a time when I was very much relying on others' wings of faith. The process of writing the meditations helped me to hear the voice of God in a very bleak wilderness.

So, having said what this work is not, let me say what it is - a reassurance that whatever we experience: confusion, frustration, pain, exhaustion; God is by our side. I have most often found this reassurance in those I term "angels" who remain by my side no matter how difficult or painful the journey, hence the dedication at the beginning of the book. It is also an attempt to explain what depression and mental health issues can feel like from a sufferer's point of view, as well as looking at the experience of the angels who walk alongside us.

Originally these meditations were not envisaged as a collection but were written as individual responses to particular difficult experiences. As the number of meditations grew, it was suggested that they were collected together as worship material suitable for Holy Week and Easter. The meditations that had already been written all seemed to reflect on the emotions of those close to Jesus during the turbulence of Holy Week, so further themes and suggestions were added to the list for exploration, and I was drawn further into the rawness and vulnerability of the final week of Jesus' life. As the  project developed, I shared it with friends to see whether it touched a chord with them, and they came back with suggestions, comments and advice. The original plan included suggested points for reflection or discussion after each meditation, the feedback from others was that this felt too directive. One very wise friend said that he had felt that all he could do in response to the strength of the emotions was to reach for a liturgy for healing and pray the opening words:

Is God our Maker here? **God is here.**
Is Christ among us? **Christ is.**
Is the Spirit here? **The life-giving Spirit is in our midst.**
And who are we? **We are God's people, redeemed by grace.**

So the directive points for reflection became a time of stillness enfolded in prayers inspired by this liturgy, and a reminder that God is with us in and through the confusion.

Another friend suggested that the focus should not be a theological question "How is God with us in confusion?" but a pastoral statement

"God is with us in confusion". The particular emphasis on mental health issues came about because I realised that many of the experiences on which I had drawn to feel the emotions of Holy Week were related to mental health issues, both as a patient and as a pastor to others. As I was drawn further into the work, I found I was comforted to know that through Holy Week when Jesus was at the centre of the turbulence, God was able to be with me in my confusion and distress. I further realised that what I wanted and needed was not an all-powerful God who could reach in and 'rescue' me to a safe place, but a God who was vulnerable and suffered alongside me, walking with me, reassuring me that this struggle could be survived.

The change of emphasis led to a new title for the project "A Voice in the Wilderness". We hear this phrase in Isaiah as a description of the messenger who tells the Exiles in Babylon that they can go home to Israel. It is also used to describe John the Baptist as he announces that the Messiah is coming. So it is associated with good news in difficult times and a message of hope. It seems apt to describe a work that aims to hear the voices of those who have struggled, and survived, to encourage others who are struggling. As we hear the emotions experienced by Jesus and those around him, we can be helped, not only by the knowledge that God was with them in their confusion, but also that they were present to witness resurrection. Thus we hear the voices of those who have survived terrible stress and strain and found a new way to live. That is why the reflections do not stop at one resurrection experience, but look at several, so that those who struggle can hear the voices speaking not only of struggle, but also of redemption and new life. It is this which can give us hope and strength to endure our own times of pain and doubt. There is a deliberate ambiguity to the subtitle "Finding God in Confusion". Holy Week is a time when we find Jesus not only surrounded by the confusion of his followers and the disciples, but also faced with his own dilemma about the agonising end to his life and the pain it would cause his friends. This means that we not only find God in our confusion but also discover that he understands it through the confusion experienced in Holy Week. Perhaps it is worth remembering that Jesus did not send the disciples away to safety, but instead allowed them to see his suffering, to see what he endured to save them and demonstrate how much he understands of their, and our, anguish.

As the disciples reflect on what is happening, they ask the same questions we do, reflecting on the Jesus they have known and his teaching and asking "Why does he do this?" and "What does he want us to do now?" In many cases I have put words into the mouths of disciples for which there is no historical evidence. I have tried to make it appropriate for what we know of them from the Gospels. We are told that James and John ask Jesus if they can sit at either side of him in glory, so I have them glorying in being on his right and left as he enters Jerusalem. I particularly wanted to give Thomas a different voice from the epithet "Doubting" so that I could explore the depth of pain and faith that led to his 'doubt'. To encompass all the emotions, I have altered the timeline of the Gospels slightly to allow Judas to witness the crucifixion in order to explore the absolute despair that led to his suicide. In some cases, I have deliberately chosen to look at the pain of those on the outside of the problem, struggling to understand what is going on, which is why there is a reflection from Thomas on Judas' betrayal, and Andrew on Peter's response to Jesus' arrest. There are also reflections on the helplessness we can feel when it seems there is nothing we can do but pray.

Throughout the work I wanted to give the message that God does not abandon us in our pain. I once heard someone preach on "being held in 'love-scarred hands'" and found it a powerful image. It gained even more significance on a visit to Basildon Park in Oxfordshire where I saw some of the initial sketches for Graham Sutherland's *Christ in Glory* tapestry for Coventry Cathedral. The hands bore the marks of the nails and yet are raised in blessing and forgiveness. In this I see the grace of God, the grace that forgives despite great disappointment

and hurt and disappointment, that bears the scars of constant love and still reaches out to embrace, that knows the cost of love and yet cannot stop loving. So I treasure the image of love-scarred hands and am encouraged that when I am scarred by loving, God understands and enfolds me and encourages me to keep loving, despite the pain.

As we travel through Holy Week and see what Jesus and his followers experienced, we listen for the voice in the wilderness that tells us that he does forgive both the pain we endure and the pain we have inflicted on others. Then when we return, in liturgy and worship to remember Jesus at the Last Supper, maybe there we will find the strength to deal with difficult and painful situations with the grace that God offers.

Although there are forty meditations in this collection, they are not intended solely for use in Lent or Holy Week, or even to be read sequentially over a set period. They have evolved into a devotional and pastoral tool for times of struggle and confusion to be selected as appropriate. As we read these meditations, memories and emotions may be stirred that are painful and difficult. I invite you to follow my friend's example, pray his prayer and find that God's voice can be heard as we offer our pain into Jesus' love-scarred hands.

Wilderness

And the Spirit immediately drove him out into the wilderness. He was in the wilderness forty days, tempted by Satan; and he was with the wild beasts; and the angels waited on him.

Mark 1:12-13

Finding God in times of wilderness and confusion is extremely difficult and painful. It is not a case of simply accepting that God has a purpose in this pain and waiting for that to become clear. It is about clinging on to faith with our finger nails whilst struggling to cope with the confusion that is raging around us. The confusion often means that all we have known and accepted as truth has been taken away from us. It can feel as if God is part of that lost certainty and therefore there is no point in looking because God is not there. Some bystanders may point out that if we can't see God, the fault is ours, not God's, but that only deepens the confusion and increases the sense of guilt that the wilderness is our fault.

Mark's stark account of Jesus' time in the wilderness begins with the statement that it was the Spirit of God who drove him there, and the implication is often drawn by preachers that the Wilderness was meant to be a fruitful time of preparation. However, it is not a helpful image for those with mental health issues. When well-meaning friends suggest that they see their 'wilderness' as a gift from God, the most likely reaction from sufferers is one of rage at God, demanding to know why they have been chosen, or a rejection of a vindictive and unloving God, or a rejection of the well-meaning friends. Whilst wrestling with a mental health episode it can be very difficult to discern which is the voice of God, and which are the voices of demons. We can become so convinced of our own worthlessness that we feel even God wants to get rid of us, especially if we are being told that God's absence is our fault, or a deliberate choice on God's part. At those times, the wild beasts will howl louder than the voices of the angels.

At such times it can be helpful to remember that Jesus was driven out into the wilderness where he had to battle wild beasts and wrestle with his faith. So the first voice we hear is that of Jesus himself, walking through the wilderness with us, empathising with our struggles and giving us the strength to keep going. We also need to hold onto the fact that Mark reassures us that there were angels with Jesus, just as there will be angels in our lives, praying for us, believing in us, walking with us, even if we don't recognise them at the time. They are the ones who wait patiently and shine the light of love and consistency into our lives.

Wild Beasts and Angels[2]

 The wilderness of despair surrounds me.
 The landscape is desolate,
 barren of life,
 barren of friends,
 no hope of escape,
 no hope at all.

 The wild beasts come to torment me.
 I do not cry out.
 No one will hear me,
 or care enough to help.
 Beasts with familiar faces,
 Doubt, Suspicion, Distrust,
 circle what little refuge I can find.

 I cannot close my eyes to them
 cannot shut out their words.
 The beasts sap my energy,
 drink dry the well of my strength
 and drain my self-worth.

 Desperate for reassurance
 I search for angels,
 but they have evaporated.
 I am alone.

I cry aloud to God
seeking answers
fullness for the emptiness
but hear only silence,
or the persistent mutterings
of the beasts.

And God sighs
and points me
to the angels who have never left me.
It is my desolation,
my isolation from my truth
who have dressed them as wild beasts.
They have their haloes still
and their wing-beats
are not drum beats of menace
but heartbeats of love.

Patiently,
never tiring of the repetition,
with gentle, tender hands
they reach into my wilderness
and call me back to fullness of life.

---

[2] *Wild Beasts and Angels* was written in 2010 at a time of great personal struggle. It was an attempt to explain how it feels to be in the grip of "demons" who destroy self-confidence and persuade us that we are worthless. It is dedicated to SJB, whose patient understanding inspired the final stanzas.

Loving God,

when wild beasts drown the voices of love and hope -
give the angels patience and understanding;

when spectres of the past overshadow the future –
give the wanderers strength and hope;

when the Wilderness seems dry and barren –
give us all courage to persevere and the faith to believe we will come to its end.

For your love's sake, AMEN

SUNDAY

a day when it all seemed so simple

1   Taking The Easy Way Out

> Then they brought the donkey to Jesus; and after throwing their cloaks on the colt, they set Jesus on it. As he rode along, people kept spreading their cloaks on the road. As he was now approaching the path down from the Mount of Olives, the whole multitude of the disciples began to praise God joyfully with a loud voice for all the deeds of power that they had seen, saying, "Blessed is the king who comes in the name of the Lord! Peace in heaven, and glory in the highest heaven!"
>
> *Luke 19:35-38*

This event is often known as the Triumphal Entry because of the way Jesus is cheered into Jerusalem by the pilgrims, who proclaim him to be the "Son of David" and "King of the Jews". It would certainly have been a great sight, to see pilgrims flocking around him, throwing their coats and palm branches onto the road to demonstrate their support of him. The pilgrims coming to Jerusalem for the Passover would have been well-versed in Jewish scripture and would have known Zechariah's prophecy that the Messiah would come on a donkey, as a symbol of peace. Were they shouting with joy that the Messiah had come, and come in peace, possibly even that it had been a bloodless revolution?

And what about the disciples? Would they have been basking in the glory of being known as one of Jesus' disciples? Were they also relieved at the apparently easy victory, that they were not going to have to suffer, that Jesus' statements about his death seemed to be wrong?

But the events of the following week show us that Jesus does not ignore suffering to take the easy way out. He knows that there is no easy way out. The only way is to acknowledge suffering and redeem it with love.

The Triumphant Procession

James: We were right beside Jesus in his victory parade.
John on his right
and me on his left.
We guided the colt
and kept back the crowds,
kicked away branches of palm
that may have tripped up its hooves.

The other disciples were in front
and behind,
waving, encouraging,
shouting to the pilgrims
only John and I were by his side.

As the pilgrims joined the parade
and shouted their "Hosannas!"
I found myself laughing with joy
and shaking with relief.

This victory was so much easier than I had thought.
There was no suffering,
no fighting,
no bloodshed,
just Jesus, coming in peace,
unnoticed by the Romans
undisturbed by the Pharisees.

He was coming to bring in a Kingdom of Peace
a Kingdom of Justice
and he was surrounded
swamped
by those who recognised his worth.
The battle was surely over
Jesus' peace had won.

I looked across to John
and saw him walking close beside Jesus,
making sure he was comfortable on the colt
keeping the crowds from pressing too close.
I caught his eye, and he smiled
a quiet smile of deep satisfaction.

This was how it was meant to be,
arriving in peace
proclaiming peace
there will be no pain
only glory
in the Kingdom of God.

I stride on, holding my head high
knowing that my brother and I will be seen
on Jesus' right and left
the disciples on whom he relies.

More pilgrims join us
pressing down from the Mount of
Olives
the psalms swell into a great chorus
and the centre of it all
are Jesus, John and me.

It is finished,
the long journey of faith is over,
there will be no more struggle for
survival
no more arguing with scribes,
no more hiding from Romans.

We have borne the sufferings with him
and come, by his side, to glory,
just as we said we would.

God our Maker, you are here.
We see you in the struggle to do right,
rather than taking the easy way to glory.

Jesus Christ, you are beside us,
understanding our desire to avoid pain for ourselves
even if it brings suffering to others.

Spirit of Light, you are within us,
giving us your strength to face the truth,
and your courage to endure suffering.

We are the People of God, held in God's everlasting arms.

2 Misunderstanding

> Then he entered Jerusalem and went into the temple; and when he had looked around at everything, as it was already late, he went out to Bethany with the twelve.
>
> *Mark 11:11*

We have all met that certain type of person who always think that they know best. They offer advice, whether it is wanted or not, and take the credit when it seems to be followed, without appearing to give any thought to the needs of the person they have advised, or their ability to think for themselves. This can be particularly frustrating when the course of action suggested is similar to one that we already have planned, but our motives for undertaking it are ignored in favour of giving credit for following advice. Our abilities and capacity for deciding our own future are discounted, and our protests and attempts at explanation are pushed aside. We are the ones with the problem, they are the ones with the solution, and in their eyes, our rôle is simply to follow advice, as if we are pawns in someone else's game.

As I reflect on Holy Week, I find myself wondering if Judas was a little like that. We know he was, or had been, linked with a revolutionary group who were desperate to overthrow Roman rule. Had he joined the disciples because he thought that Jesus was the one who would achieve this? We cannot know what his motivation was for being a follower of Jesus, but we can wonder what he felt as he saw Jesus approach Jerusalem, apparently in such commanding force. Did he believe that the revolution was about to begin?

The Wrong Revolution
Judas: I'm glad you've finally listened,
            you've followed my advice.
            You've left behind the countryside
            and headed for Jerusalem.

Don't misunderstand me,
The healings were good,
they built up a following,
earned you a name
made people listen,
but you needed to do something
you needed to make a stand
and now you have.

So the Revolution has started.
I'm surprised you chose a colt,
when a horse would have made a greater challenge.

But I suppose you thought
that pretending humility
was the best way to break in.

And we are in,
we have got into Jerusalem
without fighting,
without bloodshed,
we are in the capital city.

But why did you go to the Temple?
Why not head straight for Pilate?
We had so many following us,
so many shouting for us,
that he would have agreed to anything.

What are you afraid of?
Why won't you do it my way?
I want your new Kingdom too.
We were so close to success,
but you have just let it slip away
as we have slipped away,
back into the country,

and now we've got it all to do
again.

God our Maker, you are here,
forgiving us for thinking that we know best,
and for not giving others space to think or credit for initiative.

Jesus Christ, you are beside us,
understanding our need to be in control, and to be heard.

Spirit of Life, you are within us,
helping us to understand that your way is not our way
and that we are not always right.

We are the People of God, held in God's everlasting arms.

MONDAY

a day of surprises

3   Getting Angry

> In the temple he found people selling cattle, sheep, and doves, and the money changers seated at their tables. Making a whip of cords, he drove all of them out of the temple, both the sheep and the cattle. He also poured out the coins of the money changers and overturned their tables. He told those who were selling the doves, "Take these things out of here! Stop making my Father's house a marketplace!"
>
> *John 2: 14-16*

Reflections on this passage are often from the point of view of those who had been trading in the temple. It is easy to focus on their shock and anger at the way they were hustled out of the temple.

But how did the disciples feel? They had followed Jesus, heard his teachings on loving your enemies and your neighbours; or suggesting that we should turn the other cheek when violence is done to us; or that those who make peace are blessed. How did they feel as they watched him lashing out in rage? Had they seen him angry before? Were they shocked by his anger, or by seeing him lash out? We are not told whether or not they joined in, or simply stood by in horrified delight as Jesus took on those who had a reputation for exploiting worshippers. As they discussed it afterwards, did they remember that Jesus also preached on liberty for the captives and blessings for those who hunger and thirst for righteousness?

This passage challenges us in the same way. We are used to hearing of the God of love, of Jesus' teaching on peace and understanding, so it is a shock to hear of him getting angry and using violence. It upsets us because it seems to be out of character and does not fit easily with God accepting and forgiving us. But if we ignore it, we ignore Jesus' thirst for justice, his humanity, his feeling for those on the margins of society and his burning desire for people to know his Father, rather than the God they thought they knew through rules and rituals.

This means that living a Christian life is not always about calm acceptance, meekly submitting to whatever happens. There is a place for rage against injustice, for anger at pain, for fighting for others to be free, for letting people know that the God proclaimed by Jesus as one who brings sight to the blind and freedom for the oppressed is also interested in them.

This has particular resonance for people with mental health issues. Very often when there is a problem that causes anger or a situation that brings stress, well-meaning people give advice such as "remember that you have mental health issues" or ask, "have you taken your medication properly today?" as if the passive acceptance of a label or the swallowing of a pill is all that matters. It implies that there is nothing further to be done, anger and a thirst for freedom or justice are a waste of time and energy.

In the over-turned tables in the temple courtyard we see that there is a place for challenging accepted practice, for fighting against the system and its prejudice, and fighting for help and equality for all. It is not about swallowing anger or running away from it, but about embracing its energy and power as a force for change for the better.

Jesus, You're Really Angry!

Andrew: It took us all by surprise.
     We weren't used to seeing Jesus angry,
     Simon Peter, yes,
     he's always been quick to rage
     to speak out of turn,
     to accuse
     to lash out,
     whilst we stand aside
     and wish he'd think
     before he speaks.

     But that day,
     it was Jesus who was really angry
     and Peter who stood and watched.

We went quietly to the temple
expecting to worship
like the other pilgrims,
expecting him to teach
like every other day –
that peace,
loving your enemy
and turning the other cheek
are the way to his Kingdom.

Instead of passing by the market traders
and the money changers
as he usually did,
he stopped,
clenched his fists
and his jaw
and made a whip
from an abandoned rope.

Without warning,
he lashed out.
His whip caught a trader
who overturned his table
as he jumped with shock
and pain.

The guards moved toward him
but he stopped them
with the force of his anger
shouting the justice of his cause:
"You!"
we cowered at his rage,
"You!"
we all felt to blame,
"You have turned my Father's house

into a den of thieves!"

With a clenched fist he thumped a table
upsetting neat piles of coins
into dances of fear.

With an outstretched foot
he pushed over a stall
bursting bags of flour
causing clouds of confusion
amongst the fear.

Through it all
rang the crack of his whip
and the thunder of his voice
echoing from the walls.

"This is a holy place,
  How dare you defile it
  with your self-interest and greed?"

His face,
the loving, gentle face
we thought we knew
shone with anger
and glowed with rage.

As he overturned another table
he demanded of the terrified stall-holder:
"Why is your status, your well-being,
  more important than worship?"

We stood amazed, stunned
silenced by his passion,
battered by his words
that bounced back from these prayer-soaked walls:

"Where is God's love
  for the poor and suffering

in this closed cauldron
of self-righteous men?"

Whilst the dust settled
and Jesus went off to pray
and calm down,
we huddled in a group
and tried to make sense of it.

The way to the Kingdom
is clearly not just about submission
or calm acceptance
but is also about
shouting out
against injustice
and prejudice
and malpractice.

The way of the Kingdom
is to challenge
the selfish way of the world.

God our Maker, you are here,
forgiving us for dismissing anger and belittling passion
as unnecessary and wrong.

Jesus Christ, you are beside us,
understanding our need to ignore justice, swallow our rage,
and quieten our conscience to save ourselves trouble.

Spirit of Life, you are within us,
helping us to accept the rebuke of anger and encouraging the display
of passion,
that drive us to reassess our assumptions and discard our prejudices.

We are the People of God, fuelled by God's passion for justice.

4   Hurting Other People

> *(After Jesus had driven out the traders from the temple)* his disciples remembered that it was written, "Zeal for your house will consume me." The Jews then said to him, "What sign can you show us for doing this?" Jesus answered them, "Destroy this temple, and in three days I will raise it up." The Jews then said, "This temple has been under construction for forty-six years, and will you raise it up in three days?"
>
> *John 2: 17-20*

There can be times when we say or do things and others are hurt unintentionally and those caught up in the aftermath are often those we don't intend. We recognise the need to shout at those who have hurt us, but can be so frustrated and angry that we lash out at any one in the vicinity and hurt those who were just standing by. Seeing the pain of others who were not the target of our anger can increase our guilt at lashing out and make it hard for us to forgive ourselves for the hurt they feel. It can be hard for those who were hurt unintentionally when others lash out, particularly if they sympathise with the cause of the anger.

That is why this meditation is not written from the point of view of one of the traders in the temple whose stall was overturned, but from the point of view of a priest, who wanted only to serve God and the people. He may have agreed with Jesus' rage at the traders and been glad that someone had finally challenged them, but one of the unintended consequences would have been that with no one able to purchase sacrifices, he would not have been able to continue his vocation until order was restored. And if that were not devastating enough, the man who caused this loss was now saying that he wanted to destroy the temple altogether, and with it the priest's way of life and service.

Why Did You Hurt Me?
A Faithful Priest: Jesus,
        I understand your anger and frustration,
        your disgust with the traders
        who profit from the faithful,
        swindle the temple funds
        and exploit the poor.

        Jesus,
        I am glad you spoke your mind
        that you sent them away
        and returned the temple to God
        for prayer, for praise, for worship,
        for what it was intended.

        But your anger
        your zeal for the house of God
        has cost me my office,
        without the traders
        there is no sacrifice
        without sacrifice
        I am superfluous.

        And now,
        even though you have removed the sinners,
        and returned this house to God,
        you want to destroy the temple,
        to sever me from my vocation,
        my life's purpose to offer worship
        to forgive sins
        to comfort the grieving
        is stopped, dead.

        I am not high on the ladder of importance here,
        but I feel blessed
        to enable ordinary people to worship
        to come close to God.

You say you are the champion of the masses,
but the masses are now excluded
because they cannot offer sacrifice.
And I cannot worship,
because I cannot make that sacrifice.

No longer can I lead worship
watching patient faces turn heavenwards in prayer
clasp outstretched hands offering peace
or lead the psalms of praise
exulting as the joyful voices
rise to the rafters
or offer the reassurance after lament
to those who scream in pain.

No longer do I have the privilege
of relating the Word of God
to the reality of life,
of bringing to life God's presence
to those who have shared their life with me.

I am discarded,
unnecessary,
unwanted.

I can only stand and watch
as bewildered worshippers gather,
wondering what is happening,
questioning your purpose,
examining themselves for wrong-doing
or asking me what I have done wrong.

God gave me this vocation
and you have stolen it
leaving me empty.

God our Maker, you are here,
holding our pain,
and the pain we have caused in your healing hands.

Jesus our Saviour, you are beside us,
understanding the hurt and despair caused by acting with blind faith in
our own rightness.

Spirit of Compassion, you are here within us,
opening our eyes to the effect we have on others,
when we are so concerned with keeping to the rules that we have no
room for compassionate understanding.

We are the People of God, fuelled by God's compassion for all.

TUESDAY

a day of welcome

5   Being Wanted

Every day he was teaching in the temple. The chief priests, the scribes, and the leaders of the people kept looking for a way to kill him; but they did not find anything they could do, for all the people were spellbound by what they heard.

Luke 19:47-48

It's a relatively easy scene to picture. The crowds who have followed Jesus through the countryside, who joined the procession on Palm Sunday, have followed him into Jerusalem and to the temple. As he teaches, others come to see what the fuss is about, maybe having heard of the way Jesus has stood up to the temple authorities and cleared the way for the poor and marginalised to come back inside, or curious to see and hear the teacher about whom there has been so much talk. Away from the crowds, the temple leaders stand in a corner muttering amongst themselves about the rabble who are polluting the temple and ruining the atmosphere of this holy place.

Uncomfortably, we can find the attitude of the leaders reflected in ourselves when we are faced with people who are different from us, who long to belong, but are put off by hidden codes of behaviour they are afraid they might break. The church should be a place where hurting, broken people are welcomed and accepted, but often they feel excluded, afraid they are not good enough. They need to hear that they are welcome, that the church is a safe place in which they meet other hurting, broken people, and together find the strength to face the difficulties ahead.

You Can Come In
You have been excluded far too long
left at the threshold
looking in from the cold
longing to belong
aching with tears
of failure
and rejection
because you were told you were unclean.
You can come in,
listen
and be healed.

You have been excluded for too long
standing at the door
weeping
wanting only to share
in fellowship
to worship God.
You've seen other people,
busy,
included,
wanted,
yet when you reached out
for that closeness and value
you encountered closed doors
cold, uncaring, walls
because you've been excluded
by gender
or race
or illness
by doctrine and law.
But you can come in
listen,
know that you are valued.

You have watched with breaking hearts
not daring to come in
as those you know
have worshipped
talked, laughed,
just out of your hearing,
not turning to invite you in
but closing the door to keep you out.
But that door is now open
you can come in,
listen
you are no longer alone.

You can come in,
My Father's house
is not an exclusive place
where only the perfect can enter.
It is a place of learning
for the wise
and for the uneducated,
a place of healing
for the broken
and the whole,
a place of welcome
where the door is never shut
and everyone can worship.

You can come in,
God turns no one away.

God our Maker, you are here,
opening your arms in welcome
to those who feel left out in the cold.

Jesus Christ, you are here beside us,
understanding our need to belong
that sometimes excludes others.

Spirit of Love, you are here within us,
helping us to ignore the voices that call us to exclude others
and giving us strength to welcome those who challenge us.

We are the People of God, welcomed as treasured children.

WEDNESDAY

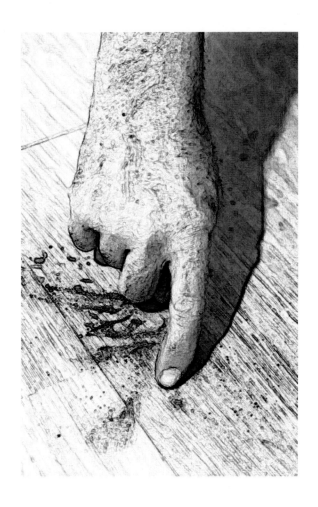

a day of acceptance

6   Feeling Ashamed

Early in the morning, Jesus came again to the temple. All the people came to him and he sat down and began to teach them. The scribes and the Pharisees brought a woman who had been caught in adultery; and making her stand before all of them, they said to him, "Teacher, this woman was caught in the very act of committing adultery. Now in the law Moses commanded us to stone such women. Now what do you say?" They said this to test him, so that they might have some charge to bring against him. Jesus bent down and wrote with his finger on the ground. When they kept on questioning him, he straightened up and said to them, "Let anyone among you who is without sin be the first to throw a stone at her." And once again he bent down and wrote on the ground. When they heard it, they went away, one by one, beginning with the elders; and Jesus was left alone with the woman standing before him.

Jesus straightened up and said to her, "Woman, where are they? Has no one condemned you?" She said, "No one, sir." And Jesus said, "Neither do I condemn you. Go your way, and from now on do not sin again."

John 8:2-11

This passage is not in every translation of John's gospel. Some translators keep it in sequence in the chapters, others put it at the end as a footnote and others omit it entirely. Whatever scholars think of its authenticity, it is a fantastic illustration of Jesus' grace and mercy. Some commentators have suggested that the woman may have been a prostitute, or that Jesus was inferring that the scribes and Pharisees may have slept with her which is why they slunk away in embarrassment, but neither interpretation is essential to understanding its main thrust. It is a warning against the pursuit of justice without mercy or being so interested in throwing the stones that we do not have compassion on the one who is condemned.

The woman was dragged before Jesus and publicly humiliated and, despite the ending to the story in the Gospel where she is told that she is not condemned, it is hard to believe that her neighbours or her accusers would have let her forget her humiliation easily. She would have gained a certain reputation that it would be hard to lose.

It can be a similar experience for those with mental health issues, who gain a reputation for irrational behaviour and are no longer afforded the respect offered to others. They can feel condemned without trial or understanding or the opportunity to explain their actions. The community around them can find it hard to let go of the image of irrational behaviour and they are stigmatised, just as the woman may have been stigmatised for her behaviour. And some members of the community condemn from the fear that they may suffer mental health problems themselves. They throw the stones of exclusion and ridicule to conceal their own struggles.

This passage is a reminder that no one is perfect, and that we should have compassion on the flaws of others rather than gathering stones with which to persecute them. And, most importantly, that with God, there are endless opportunities to try again.

Does No One Condemn You?
I was betrayed by someone I trusted,
who loved me and whom I enfolded in love,
someone who said they understood
and encouraged me to share my secrets,
before shattering my trust
to save themselves from blame.

I was left naked
vulnerable
to the eyes
and gossip
of my neighbours.

This Rabbi was different.
They dragged me in front of him

expecting my downfall
but received instead his censure.
In the face of his gentleness and compassion
and searing insight
they melted away.

And he smiled at me
and his smile reached his eyes,
unlike others,
who claimed to be there for me
whilst reaching for the stones
with which I would be punished
and quoting the law
by which I would be condemned.

He did not judge me,
he showed me mercy
and compassion.
He wanted to set me free
but I still face their condemnation
and vengeance
for the stones they did not throw.

Now people whisper and speculate,
walking past with averted eyes,
shooting me sideways looks
and knowing glances.
Conversations stop
and I feel the frostiness in the air
as heavy and painful as the stones they didn't throw.

Friends are withdrawing
"She'll understand" they say.
I don't.

All I know is shame and despair,
weighing me down

and walling me in.
I know that I am despised,
for weakness
for stepping outside what is expected.
I see it in people's eyes
before they slide away from me
pretending not to have looked
not to have seen.

The stones of their condemnation
hang heavily around my neck.
They were not hurled at me
but the accusations were
and they fill my ears
although my accusers have gone away.

The stones of rejection
weigh down my heart
as those who once called themselves my friends
turn away
afraid to be seen
with someone with my reputation,
as if my behaviour is contagious
and I will lead them astray

The stones of prejudice
slow my steps
and hinder my progress.
I am given no chance to explain.
No one is willing to listen,
saying they've had "enough of my lies".
The courtesy shown to others
is denied to me
because of who I am
and how they think I behave.
They think I do not feel

that I do not understand,
and that therefore
I do not matter.

Strangers who do not know me
or of what I am accused
treat me with kindness and courtesy.
They are viewed by those in the know
with patronising sympathy
and incredulous outrage.
At the first opportunity
my detractors
detach them from my company
and make sure they do not return.

Where now is the compassion of that Rabbi?
Where now the love I once knew?
The stones pile heavily over my heart
preventing love and trust
from ever escaping again.

God our Maker, you are here,
forgiving us for the stones we store up to hurl at others.

Jesus our Redeemer, you are here,
understanding why we want to hurt others when we are hurting.

Spirit of Compassion, you are here within us,
helping us to let go of our hurt and our guilt
and heal our wounds.

We are God's People, forgiven and free of condemnation.

7   When We Are Misunderstood

> One of the Pharisees asked Jesus to eat with him, and he went into the Pharisee's house and took his place at the table. And a woman in the city, who was a sinner, having learned that he was eating in the Pharisee's house, brought an alabaster jar of ointment. She stood behind him at his feet, weeping, and began to bathe his feet with her tears and to dry them with her hair. Then she continued kissing his feet and anointing them with the ointment. Now when the Pharisee who had invited him saw it, he said to himself, "If this man were a prophet, he would have known who and what kind of woman this is who is touching him—that she is a sinner."
>
> *Luke 7: 36-39*

There are several suggestions about who this woman might be.   Luke does not give her a name, saying only that she is a repentant sinner. Some traditional interpretations have suggested that she is Mary Magdalene, repenting of her former life. In John's version of this story she is Mary, sister of Martha and of Lazarus whom Jesus had raised from the dead. According to John's interpretation, Mary's action is one of gratitude for restoring her brother's life. Matthew and Mark tell a slightly different story in which a woman anoints Jesus' head with perfume, as if preparing him for death. Luke may well have pulled together two stories, of a repentant sinner who comes into a public place and weeps over Jesus' feet before hurriedly wiping them dry with her hair, and the way Mary anointed Jesus before his death.

In all versions of the story, the woman's action attracts criticism. In John's gospel she is criticised by Judas for her extravagant gesture, suggesting that the ointment should have been sold and the money given to the poor. In Luke's version she is judged for who she is, and Jesus is criticised for not rejecting her. As the story continues, he turns

the criticism on his host who had not offered the traditional hospitality of washing feet that would have been dusty from the road, and also for scoffing at the woman who has done it in his place. Maybe the woman's critics were embarrassed into self-defence knowing that they took generosity for granted and rarely remembered to express their thanks as she was doing, or they were jealous of the attention she was getting for her generosity and were frustrated that they had not been the ones to take the initiative.

Luke's version of the story echoes with my experience of offering gifts of friendship and gratitude to people who have accompanied me on difficult journeys. Sometimes they are rejected or misunderstood with criticism for over-generosity, just as Judas criticised Mary for her extravagance. But that misses the point. These gifts are not to showcase the generosity of the giver or to embarrass others into doing the same, they are gifts from a heart overflowing with love because someone has bothered to take time, to listen, to care, to value the giver.

A Gift of Love
He had changed my life.
At my lowest point
he turned and listened
when others turned away.
He understood my struggles
when others put the blame on me
for not trying hard enough.

He smiled,
he valued me,
he listened
when others shouted me down
and smiled without their eyes
or their hearts.

So I just had to thank him
to show him how much he meant,
because he had valued me,

and encouraged me
to value myself.

I heard that he was in town,
so I took my courage in both hands,
found the most precious thing I had,
and went to find him.
The size of the house daunted me
the number of people outside
almost made me turn back.

Then I remembered
his smile
his gentle touch,
his encouragement,
and I pushed my way through.

I ignored the hostile stares,
the accusations,
the harsh remarks,
focussing only on my mission,
to thank my saviour
from the bottom of my heart.

I knelt in tears over his feet,
tears that washed away
the cares and toil of the day
just as he had washed away
the cares and toil
of years of self-condemnation.

I had forgotten a towel,
so I wiped his feet with my hair
and anointed them with my perfume,
and only then found the courage
to look up into his eyes
and saw love and understanding

and gratitude for my care.

The bubble burst
and I could hear critical voices
complaining at my extravagance
and intrusion into their seclusion.

At first I was ashamed
and then I was filled with anger.
I wanted to turn and scream at them
"Just because you have never felt excluded
  and felt your heart explode with love
  and gratitude
  when someone listens
  and pours understanding into your life
  instead of scorn,
  don't judge me
  when I need to say thank you'!"

They judged my outpouring of love
as "wasteful" and "sinful".
How can the overflowing of love
be sinful or wasteful?
It was a 'just because' gift
Not planned to get something in return
or designed to get public recognition or thanks
like so many of their gifts.
It was just because
he understood.

God our Maker, you are here,
pouring love into our hearts,
that overflows to engulf others.

Jesus Christ, you are here,
understanding our offerings of love,
even when others scoff or turn us away.

Spirit of Life, you are here within us,
helping us to express our thanks
and to receive gifts of love without guilt or condemnation.

We are God's People, loved and cherished, whatever we have to offer.

THURSDAY

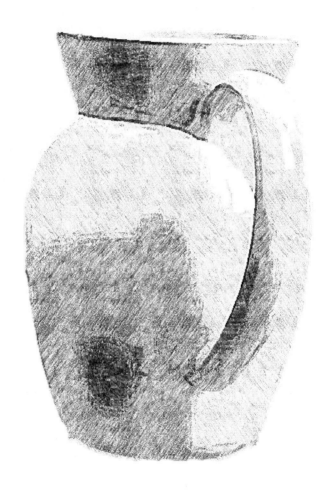

a day of bewilderment

8   When We Are Too Proud

Jesus got up from the table, took off his outer robe, and tied a towel around himself. Then he poured water into a basin and began to wash the disciples' feet and to wipe them with the towel that was tied around him.

John 13:3-5

It was a simple job to do, going round and cleaning people's feet, refreshing them after a day on hot and dusty roads. No one wanted to do it because it was not a pleasant job and it was menial, something that servants did. So Jesus does the unexpected and demonstrates that there is no job too small to matter to God, and no one too important to do it. It takes his disciples by surprise, and they are ashamed when they realise that their pride has blinded them to the message of the Kingdom.

We all have times when we think that menial tasks are beneath us, or that we are too important to be bothered by other people's needs. So we turn a blind eye and hope they will go away, just as the disciples hoped that someone else would deal with the problem of the unwashed feet. Or there are jobs that we are unwilling to do because they are not pleasant, the conversation about whether an elderly person is capable of living on their own, or the breaking of difficult or bad news. We prefer to let others do the jobs, even when they are our responsibility, so that we can avoid the pain and trouble they will cause us.

I Should Have Done That

Philip: There was no servant waiting when we went in,
           There was a bowl, and a towel
           but no one standing with it
           waiting to clean our feet.

           We all looked at one another
           one or two looked pointedly at me
           as if it was my turn.

61

But why should it be?
Washing other people's feet is not pleasant,
it's a dirty job,
that none of us wanted to do.

Looking back,
I ask myself why?
Why didn't I do it?
Why didn't I wash their feet?
I could have done,
we all could have done
but we didn't.

I could have picked up the bowl and towel,
but why should I?
I didn't want the others to think I am less than they are
I am already different because I am Greek,
not allowed into their precious temple,
teased for being a Gentile,
why should I be the one to wallow
in the dirt and rubbish of the floor
and wash more off their feet?
It's a servant's job.

So I ignored the hints
the unspoken expectation
that I would do it
that it was my responsibility
and joined loudly in the conversation of the others
about the festival
the teaching in the temple
and James' latest theory about the Kingdom.
I could have washed their feet,
But it's a servant's job
to grovel before others,
not the job of a follower of Jesus.

We were all hungry
and anxious for the meal to start,
so we were relieved when at last,
a servant appeared with a towel round his waist
and began to wash our feet.
He came to me and I didn't look down
I just carried on arguing with Thomas
about where we should sit at the table.

I noticed that the servant's touch was gentle
and that he was thorough
not the usual quick sluice of water
and brusque rub with the towel,
but I was determined not to notice him.

It was only when Peter pushed him away
and loudly declared
that he would not have his feet washed by him
that we turned to look at the cause of the commotion.
The room fell silent with our shame,
we looked at the floor
unable to speak
not daring to meet each other's eyes.

It was not a servant who had washed our feet
but the Master.
He was not too proud to wallow in the dirt
and to wash the same off our feet.

He was not too proud
to do the servant's job.
And he had done it without fuss
without drawing attention to himself.
That was his way.

All I could think was
"I could have done it."

"I should have done it."
I knew that I should have done the dirty work
rather than leaving it to someone else.
I didn't do it, because I was too proud.
Like the others, I was deeply ashamed.

And when we faltered back into speech
and protested that we were about to do it
that we were just going to pick up the towel
and kneel on the floor,
he looked at us,
and knew us for the proud, weak,
self-centred people we are.

He knew we weren't 'about to do it'.
He knew we were fooling no one but ourselves.
He knew we didn't want the dirty job
didn't want to be uncomfortable
or taken for granted by others.

With the heavy smile we had come to know
he reminded us that his Kingdom is not about hierarchy
but service,
that the first shall be last and the last, first,
that we should not let pride
or concern for our status
stop us from serving others in love.

God our Maker, you are here,
forgiving us our pride, our concern for the opinions of others.

Jesus Christ, you are here beside us,
understanding why we are reluctant to do the unpleasant jobs,
and why we try to hide our guilt behind feeble excuses.

Spirit of Truth, you are here within us,
prompting us to admit our failings
and giving us strength to overcome them.

We are God's People, washed and refreshed by God's love.

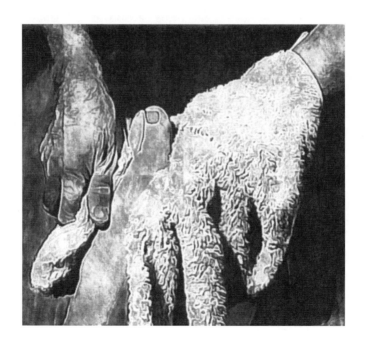

9   Betrayal

While they were eating, he said, "Truly I tell you, one of you will betray me." And the disciples became greatly distressed and began to say to him one after another, "Surely not I, Lord?" He answered, "The one who has dipped his hand into the bowl with me will betray me."

Matthew 26:21-23

Betrayal is hard to understand because it so completely alters our view and understanding of someone. We question all we have ever known about them. Most of all we question ourselves, whether the trust we have put in others is misplaced and should be withdrawn to avoid the possibility of further hurt. But Jesus' action in the Upper Room, including Judas, including the rest of the disciples who would betray his trust in other ways, shows us that we do need to let go of the bitterness of betrayal, and forgive ourselves for misunderstanding and forgive others for letting us down.

In grappling with the many questions arising from betrayal, this meditation has moved between being written in the first person, expressing Jesus' deep grief at Judas' betrayal, and in the third person showing the other disciples' incredulity that one of their own could betray Jesus, and their struggle to understand why he has changed. Both points of view are powerful, and both have potential to speak to contemporary experience of friendship and betrayal. It finally settled into the third person, allowing for a reflection on why Jesus would not retaliate. This may also resonate with the experience of bewildered bystanders when marriages collapse, common principles seem to be denied or a close friendship suddenly come to an end, and they look at someone they thought they knew and ask "Why?"

How Could You Do This?

Thomas to Judas:
>I cannot believe it,
>none of us
>loyal friends,
>loyal to Jesus,
>loyal to each other,
>could ever betray him.

>But when you dip your bread with him,
>I see in your eyes
>and in the hardness of your mouth
>that he has disappointed you,
>let you down,
>hurt your pride
>not fulfilled your hopes.

>But did it have to come to this?
>this public shunning
>this open rejection
>of all that he is
>of all that we have shared
>of all that he represents?

>The pain is sharp as a sword
>piercing straight to my heart
>where we have held you
>and treasured you.

>Will I ever get over this pain
>that twists and constricts my heart
>whenever I remember
>how much we cared for you,
>welcomed you, included you,
>trusted you,
>loved you?

Will I ever break the habit
of turning to you
to share triumph
or disaster?
Or reaching out to care for you
when I see you struggling?
Or of stepping between you
and the wrath of others?

Can I ever break the habit of friendship
nurtured through fire and laughter
strength and vulnerability
on both sides?

And can I ever trust again
that such friendship is needed
wanted,
valued?

I look at the sea of shocked faces
and though I know them
it would be so easy to distrust
them now
to avoid being close
to escape the need for honesty
and evade the risk
of future betrayal and pain
that twists
and colours every memory
taints every shared pleasure
and makes me question my judgement.

For how long did you hate him?
For how long have you been plotting
and planning his downfall?
When did friendship end
overwhelmed by loathing?

When was constant faith
superseded by self-interest
and loyalty by expediency?

When did he cease to matter?
When did his hurt, his feelings, his integrity
become things of indifference
replaced by your need for approval
your desire to succeed
your need to blame others
to escape blame yourself?

Yet though you are ready to betray the promises
the confidences of friendship
I cannot.
Whatever pain I feel
I cannot betray your trust
or your vulnerability,
even though I know
you will betray mine.

Promises are meant to be kept
trust treasured
and confidences held secure.

I do not understand what you are doing
or what has led you here.
The pain is unstoppable.
I cannot withhold
the bitterness of betrayal
and destroyed hope.
Looking into his eyes,
I see not anger
but anguish and suffering
caused by your change of heart.

I think of his teaching to turn the other cheek

and know that he will not retaliate.
I remember him telling Peter
to forgive seventy times seven
and I know that he will not apportion blame
because that is not the way of God.

He will take your bitterness
accept the consequences
of your broken promises
and sweeten and fill them
with love.

He will still love you
to death.

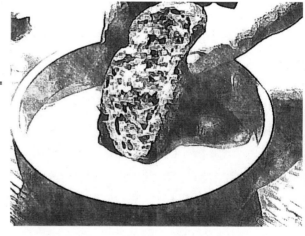

*God our Maker,
you are here,
forgiving us for the
ways in which we
betray our friends.*

*Jesus our Redeemer,
you are here beside
us,
understanding why we lose faith and hope when we are betrayed
and the depth of pain that betrayal inflicts.*

*Spirit of Compassion, you are here within us,
helping us to understand why we have been betrayed
and to forgive those who have wounded us so deeply.*

*We are God's People, forgiven, understood and held in love-scarred
hands.*

10   Forgiving The Hurt

> Then he took a loaf of bread, and when he had given thanks, he broke it and gave it to them, saying, "This is my body, which is given for you. Do this in remembrance of me." And he did the same with the cup after supper, saying, "This cup that is poured out for you is the new covenant in my blood.
>
> *Luke 22:19-20*

The point at which I find Jesus' compassion and God's grace most forcibly demonstrated is the place to which all Christians return in liturgy and worship – the Last Supper. With his disciples he celebrated the Passover, a festival that celebrates the moment in history when God's people became supremely aware that they worshipped a living God who was intervening to save them from oppression.   Jesus uses that significance to remind his disciples that salvation comes not through our own strength, but through the grace of God, who brings forgiveness and reconciliation. It is on God's initiative that the New Covenant will be sealed, and through God's initiative, through God's broken body and outpoured blood that we will find New Life.

The Gospels make it clear that even though he knew that his disciples would let him down causing him unimaginable pain and anguish, Jesus still welcomed them at his table to celebrate the Passover and included them in the wine of the New Covenant.   I find this incredible.   Our natural instinct is to protect ourselves and turn away people who have hurt us, yet Jesus included them, and includes us who also let him down, at the greatest celebration of grace there can ever be.

And he gave the instruction "Do this, to remember me." It is not only in the breaking of the bread and sharing of wine that we remember him, but in the act of welcoming those who hurt, including those who betray and drawing in those who desert.

Do This, To Remember Me

Philip: "Do this, to remember me" he said
  Why did he choose this moment,
  this sacred feast,
  to issue that instruction?

  He taught us so much
  about the loving God
  who welcomes the home-comers
  and looks for the lost.

  He has shown us so much courage,
  by confronting the strong
  and challenging the powerful.

  He has demonstrated generosity
  by welcoming children when he was tired
  and feeding thousands from one small meal.

  He even let us witness his divinity
  – when he was transfigured by light
  and when he walked on water.

  But at none of these did he say
  "Do this to remember me."

  He said it at a meal table,
  over bread and wine,
  the everyday things
  of everyday meals.

  Is this it?
  Nothing spectacular,
  Only the everyday?
  There is nothing special
  about breaking bread
  and drinking wine.

We wanted something spectacular
something that would demonstrate to others
that we really knew you.

And I wish you had waited until Judas had gone.
If you already knew he was going,
why let him spoil it?

Or is that what you really meant?
Not the ordinariness of the bread and wine,
or the everyday action of eating a meal,
but that every day,
we must kneel
with those who hurt and desert us,
who take the easy way out,
who wilfully misunderstand us
to achieve their own purpose?

"Do this,
   share, tolerate,
   forgive and redeem
   to remember me."

God our Maker, you are here,
offering us hope and new life in everyday things.

Jesus our Redeemer, you are here beside us,
knowing the sins that we are tempted to commit,
and that they will grieve us as much as they grieve you.

Spirit of Grace, you are here within us,
helping us to forgive others
and giving us the courage to forgive ourselves.

We are God's People, forgiven and renewed by the love of God.

11   Letting People Down

> Then Jesus went with them to a place called Gethsemane; and he said to his disciples, "Sit here while I go over there and pray." He took with him Peter and the two sons of Zebedee, and began to be grieved and agitated. Then he said to them, "I am deeply grieved, even to death; remain here, and stay awake with me."
> Then he came to the disciples and found them sleeping; and he said to Peter, "So, could you not stay awake with me one hour?"
>
> *Matthew 26: 36-38, 40*

How must Peter have felt at Jesus' words?   "So, could you not stay awake with me one hour?" He had let down his Master, the man he had followed through thick and thin for the last three years. It seemed to be such a simple thing, to sit there and stay awake, but the disciples were tired, their eyes were heavy with sleep after eating a large meal and when sleep overtook them, they did not fight it. They did not know, could not understand the importance of praying with Jesus until it was too late.

We have all been in situations where we feel that we have let people down, by not doing what we have promised, by failing to remember important details or by simply falling asleep and not being there when we are needed. It makes us feel guilty, annoyed with ourselves, or annoyed with someone else for not reminding us. In our guilt and annoyance, we make excuses to explain away our failure, blaming others, particularly the one we have let down by saying they should have explained more clearly what they needed or expected.

The experience of letting someone down is common for those caring for someone with mental health issues. It is not always easy to understand why small things, like returning phone calls; consistency of response; clear explanations of changes of plan; remembering to use a person's chosen name; or keeping promises are so important. Small things that are accidentally forgotten can suddenly be magnified to matters of almost life and death leaving the carer at sea in a fog of anger and guilt. Carers can be bewildered by situations that have not been a problem in the past, or with which the other person seems to have been coping recently without problems. And when something goes seriously wrong, the carer wonders if it was their fault, and whether things would have been different if they had only kept their promise, and their head can be full of "if only I hadn't said" or "if only I'd tried harder", or "was it really that important?".

Was It Really That Important?
Peter: Was it really that important
         for us to stay awake?
         You have understood in the past
         when we've got it wrong,
         when we've failed
         because we were tired
         or because we didn't understand.
         You always gave us another chance
         always patiently explained
         why it mattered
         what we should have done.

But this time
when a busy day
and an exhausting journey
overtook us,
you were angry,
you did not explain.
You shouted
and frightened us.

Was it really that important, this time?
What has changed?
You were praying.
You've never needed us to stay awake before.
Why is it different now?

Was it really that important
for you to know that we were awake
that we were watching your agony?
It was hard to fight sleep
with a full stomach
and heavy eyes.
We only slept for a moment
but it was the moment
that you came back.

You knew we were tired!
You knew we couldn't stay awake!
Yet you were angry with us!

Was it really that important
that we prayed?
I've said that you are the Messiah
you are the Son of God.
You were praying,
what difference would our prayers have made?
God listens to you,
we couldn't have changed anything!

If it really was that important
then I'm sorry, Lord,
sorry I've let you down,
sorry, I didn't understand.

God our Maker, you are here,
forgiving us for letting down our friends
and for blaming others for letting us down.

Jesus our Redeemer, you are here beside us,
understanding why we magnify small things to great importance
and why it bewilders others.

Spirit of Compassion, you are here within us,
helping us to understand how we have upset others
and quietening the questions that plague our minds.

We are God's People, fallible and forgiven by our loving God.

12 Wishing It Would Go Away

Going a little farther, he threw himself on the ground and prayed, "My Father, if it is possible, let this cup pass from me; yet not what I want but what you want."

Again he went away for the second time and prayed, "My Father, if this cannot pass unless I drink it, your will be done."

Matthew 26: 39, 42

This passage has clear resonance with our human response to struggle and challenge. We hear our desire for someone to take away the suffering, for time to rewind so that the disaster can be avoided, or for it all to be over, echoed in Jesus' plea to "let this cup pass away from me." It describes so vividly our emotions when faced with seemingly impossible or unbearably painful situations. In Jesus' resigned words of acceptance "not my will, but yours be done", we hear his realisation that the only way to heal the situation is to accept the excruciating pain of seeing it through to the end. At any point in the following hours he could have defended himself and given himself an opportunity to walk away from the pain, but he stayed with the way of love that he had accepted was the only way. Through it we see his incredible strength and faith, and his compassion for those caught up in the suffering with him.

For anyone who is overwhelmed by painful or challenging circumstances the feeling of 'not again' and 'why won't it just go away?' are uncomfortably familiar, as is "let this cup pass away" in the form of "Why me?" or "Why am I the only one who suffers, isn't it someone else's turn?" People on the outside fail to understand the reality within which we are living when they try to comfort us with suggestions that "God will use our suffering for good" or that "God has something special for us when it's all over". Another way they demonstrate their lack of understanding is when they try to encourage us to see that other people are worse off so that we get things into perspective When we are mired in the bleakness of the pain and grief, the future is the next minute or the next hour, not the next day or week or month or some vague "happier time" to come. From behind the barriers of survival and struggle, it is impossible to consider others' experience in order to count our blessings or to understand someone else's pain when we are drowning in our own. And the feeling of failure, that we are not coping, that it is all our fault increases because we can't "get over it" on our own.

Here in Gethsemane as Jesus prays alone, we eavesdrop on his vulnerability, his fear of what lies ahead, and his very human response to the prospect of unimaginable pain. His pleas to God to be spared, for there to be another way, reassure us that in our agonies and our temptations to walk away from distressing situations, he is with us, understanding our fears and holding us in his love-scarred hands as we wrestle with impossible choices.

Let This Cup Pass Away From Me

The mind races with questions
scrabbling for understanding
for reason,
for a reason,
for any reason,
to keep going.

Why is this happening?
Why me, again?
What have I done
that I have to face this,
digging deep into exhausted resources
and finding non-existent strength
to face pain I don't want.

I cannot see beyond now
to the other side of this excruciating pain.
I cannot understand why it has to be like this.

Surely there must be a better way

to achieve the same end,
if there is a plan
if there is something at the end
that makes this worth enduring,
I cannot believe that this agony
is the only way to achieve it,
the only route to the good beyond,
if that good even exists.

Is it so wrong
to want to walk away
to leave this behind,
forget the demands of love
and the deep scar of grief?
Why is it failure
to want peace
in place of pain?

I want only peace
and a respite from questions,
a respite from pain.
I want this cup to pass me by,
this poison to be on someone else's lips,
whilst mine taste the sweetness of yesterday,
instead of the bitterness of today
that lingers into too many tomorrows.
O God, let this cup pass me by,
please.

*God our Maker, you are here,
forgiving us for wanting to walk away from the pain we have to face,
and for feeling overwhelmed by our responsibilities.*

*Jesus our Redeemer, you are here beside us,
understanding our dread of pain and difficult paths
and helping us to find a way through them.*

*Spirit of Compassion, you are here within us,
giving us the strength we need
to take each agonising step
and staying with us to the very end.*

*We are God's People, fallible and forgiven by
our loving God and surrounded by love that
understands our pain.*

13   When We Are Deceived

> While he was still speaking, Judas, one of the twelve, arrived; with him was a large crowd with swords and clubs, from the chief priests and the elders of the people.
> Now the betrayer had given them a sign, saying, "The one I will kiss is the man; arrest him." At once he came up to Jesus and said, "Greetings, Rabbi!" and kissed him.
>
> *Matthew 26: 47-49*

This was the moment Judas' betrayal became real, when he publicly changed from a supporter of Jesus to an opposer, someone who was looking to destroy him. Far more than anxiety for his disciples, or fear of what was to come for him, the knowledge that someone he had trusted was the catalyst for pain, must have been unbearably difficult. And to be betrayed with a kiss of welcome and peace must have been the ultimate insult.

It can be a similar experience when caring for someone with mental health issues, when they suddenly reject the care they have previously accepted, or when they self-harm or become suicidal. It can feel as if all our effort and concern is being thrown back at us, a betrayal of love and compassion.

And for those with mental health issues, there are those we encounter who encourage us to trust them, and then lead us into trouble with no warning. They are like wolves in sheep's clothing, befriending us, not out of compassion, but for the approval of their goodness by others; or for what they can gain in glory when we are 'healed' by them; or because they think we are easy to manipulate, giving them a sense of power. Having earned our trust and friendship, they discover that our needs are too complex, and they walk away, blaming us for their failure. And the betrayal hurts.

Betrayed With A Kiss
To Judas:

You came with soft words
that spoke of care
and loyalty.
But your eyes
unable to meet his,
looking instead to those behind you
for approval,
revealed your true feelings.

Your heart was full
of apprehension
for what you were about to do
and how he would react.

You were fearful
of where this would lead,
but more afraid of the crowd
and their reaction
if you failed them now.

You offered the kiss of peace,
the kiss of blessing and goodwill -
but if you had truly wanted that
you would have trusted him
talked to him
listened to him -
rather than turning against him
too afraid to go against the crowd,
your new best friends,
who were egging you on.

Had you trusted him,
had you listened,
that kiss of peace
would not signal the end,

but the beginning,
a new start
renewed compassion
and understanding.

But you gave in
you turned away from compassion.
So your kiss of peace
is now a kiss of death.

God our Maker, you are here,
forgiving us when we lose faith in others or ourselves.

Jesus our Redeemer, you are here beside us,
understanding the stabbing pain
when we are rejected and let down by others.

Spirit of Grace,
you are here within us,
helping us to let go of the pain
and regret of trusting the wrong
person.

We are God's People,
held in our pain
and cherished despite our
brokenness.

14　Over-reacting

When those who were around him saw what was coming, they asked, "Lord, should we strike with the sword?" Then one of them struck the slave of the high priest and cut off his right ear. But Jesus said, "No more of this!" And he touched his ear and healed him.

Luke 22:49-51

Although he is not named in Luke's Gospel, according to John it was Peter who lashed out and cut off the servant's ear. It fits with the image of Peter that has been built up over the centuries – an impetuous, outspoken man who often acted without thinking, driven by passion and instinct rather than reflection and restraint. This meditation is written from the point of view of Andrew as Peter's brother, probably an older brother who was used to Peter's unpredictability and spent a large part of his life looking after him and calming him down before he exploded. He understood that when Peter was hurting and frightened, he lashed out, needing to hurt others to alleviate his own pain. He also knew how much Jesus meant to Peter, and how protective his brother could be of those whom he loved. So Andrew would not be surprised that Peter drew his sword without thinking of the consequences. It is a scenario familiar to carers of people with mental health issues, being prepared for unpredictability and ready to take action to protect those they love.

Lashing Out

Andrew:　　Peter has always lashed out,
　　　　　　expressing his feelings
　　　　　　with volume
　　　　　　and energy.

　　　　　　He did it as a child,
　　　　　　screaming over the least injustice
　　　　　　or when he was forbidden
　　　　　　what he most wanted.

With time,
he learned to control it,
to bite his tongue,
to be more tolerant.
It made life easier,
for him,
and for me.

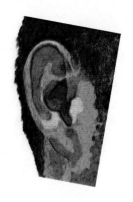

As his older brother,
I no longer had to watch him
waiting for the next eruption
wondering what he would do next.

He still had times
when his anger boiled over
so that he just had to do something,
anything,
to let people know how he was feeling.
Mostly now he just shouts
or speaks without thinking.

It can be embarrassing
when he says aloud
what we are all thinking
or when he behaves
like a petulant child,
unhappy at being left out
or getting the answer wrong.

But tonight,
he really boiled over
exploding with rage,
frustration,
and confusion.

He was so confused,
so angry, so hurt

that he didn't speak -
he lashed out
with a sword.

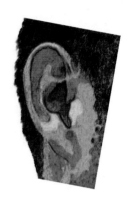

He wanted to defend his friend
to save him from hurt
to keep him from harm.

He didn't see the hordes
with cudgels and spears
standing near
ready to react,
to arrest.

He didn't think of his own danger.
He saw only our leader,
surrounded,
in danger,
and lashed out
to save him.

I suffered with him,
I too wanted to lash out
to fight back.
My arm twitched
as his swept out
and cut off the ear
of an innocent bystander.

I wasn't close enough to stop him
to console him
to tear him away
strong arms around him
pulling him from danger
as I've done so many times.

I could only stand in horror
as the blood flowed

as my brother showed
his anger
his frustration
at his impotence.

I understood
but I wished and prayed
he had learned
to hold his tongue
to swallow his temper
to wait and see
rather than rush in
and act.

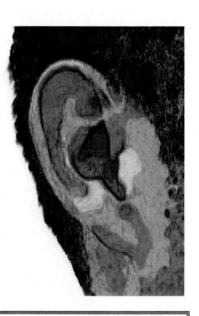

I understood,
but I wept
for his despair
and my own.

God our Maker, you are here,
forgiving us for lashing out because we are hurting.

Jesus Christ, you are here beside us,
understanding our frustration and unpredictability.

Spirit of Truth, you are here within us,
helping us to understand why we lash out
and giving us the patience to keep control of our actions.

We are God's People, fallible and forgiven by our loving God.

15 Denial

Then they seized him and led him away, bringing him into the high priest's house. But Peter was following at a distance. When they had kindled a fire in the middle of the courtyard and sat down together, Peter sat among them. Then a servant-girl, seeing him in the firelight, stared at him and said, "This man also was with him." But he denied it, saying, "Woman, I do not know him."

A little later someone else, on seeing him, said, "You also are one of them." But Peter said, "Man, I am not!"

Then about an hour later still another kept insisting, "Surely this man also was with him; for he is a Galilean." But Peter said, "Man, I do not know what you are talking about!" At that moment, while he was still speaking, the cock crowed.

The Lord turned and looked at Peter.

Luke 22:54-61a

Denial by friends and family is extremely painful. We ask ourselves why they have ignored us, or what we have done to upset them, or why they no longer think us worthy of friendship or loyalty. We search for reasons in our behaviour to explain this lack of faith or friendship and try to defend their actions to ourselves by suggesting that they had our best interests at heart. When we realise that the truth of the denial is that they do not wish to know us, or do not want to take the trouble to understand us or walk with us in our struggle, the anguish of denial can become as heart-breaking as that of betrayal, as we regret the previous closeness and the secrets we have shared which may now be made public. Yet despite knowing the pain it causes, denial is such an easy trap into which to fall that it happens almost without our realising it, and we try to explain it away to ourselves and to anyone who will listen.

In this scene we see things from Peter's perspective. He was desperate to know what had happened to Jesus, so followed him and the guards at a distance and tried to hide himself in the crowds that had gathered around the fire. But his appearance and his accent gave him away as a Galilean and he was challenged to acknowledge that he was a disciple of Jesus.

We can all identify with Peter's dilemma. He wanted to remain loyal to Jesus, but he could not be sure whether those around him were hostile or sympathetic to Jesus' teaching. He was afraid that if he admitted that he was one of Jesus' followers, he would be dragged into the trial with him, and possibly face the same fate. In the pressure of the moment, he chose denial. It may even have slipped out before he realised what he was saying, and then he had to decide whether to continue with the lie or own up to being one of the Twelve. Once a lie has been told, it is so much easier to continue with it, than to confess the truth, so Peter denied Jesus not just once, but three times. As he realised what he had done, he may have tried to reason it out, to persuade himself that the denials were a means to an end, whilst realising from Jesus' look that he had let down his Lord.

I Denied Him!

Peter: I've just denied him!
    I've followed him for three years
    given up my family
    my home
    my inheritance
    everything.
    I have been utterly loyal,
    and yet
    I've just denied knowing him.

    Did I do it to save my own skin?
    Am I afraid of the repercussions
    or that it will reflect badly on me?
    What will he think?

I've denied him again
The lie was easier this time
because it was to save him.
If I stay free,
avoid arrest,
I can help him, save him.
Yes,
if I'm not arrested,
I can round up the others -
show how much he is loved,
prove his innocence.
He'll never know I denied him
when it comes right in the end.

I've denied him a third time,
I even swore an oath
to make it convincing.
I denied him to save him.
Denying him was the right thing to do
the right thing
to achieve what he wants,
to bring in his Kingdom
of justice
and truth.
He'll never know that I lied
to save him.

He knows I've denied him.
As he was dragged past me,
He looked at me,
through me,
into me,
right into my heart.

He knows I've denied him,
not to save him,

but to save myself.

The cock is crowing!
Jesus was right.
He knows me so well!
I hear his voice
"Before the cock crows
  You will deny me."

I see his eyes
looking into my soul
knowing my selfishness.

He knew all along
knew that I would fail him
knew that I would be weak
and frightened.

The cock is crowing again.
I wish I was dead.
What have I done?
Lord, what have I done?

God our Maker, you are here,
forgiving us for giving in to the instinct for self-preservation.

Jesus Christ, you are here beside us,
understanding why we deny our friends and take the easy way out.

Spirit of Life, you are here within us,
helping us to stop hiding from ourselves and acknowledge the truth.

We are God's People, fallible and weak, but still loved and held by God.

16   When There Are Only Tears

The Lord turned and looked at Peter.
Then Peter remembered the word of the Lord, how he had said to him, "Before the cock crows today, you will deny me three times."

And he went out and wept bitterly.

Luke 22: 61-62

This scene follows on immediately from Peter's denial, which closed with a sudden change of perspective from Peter to Jesus. He came out of the courthouse and was confronted with Peter in the courtyard denying him. Luke only says that "the Lord turned and looked at Peter" so we are left to imagine what that look contained, sorrow, grief, disappointment, regret, hurt? And this was only hours after Peter had been rebuked for sleeping whilst Jesus needed him to pray. Was Peter then overwhelmed with a feeling of hopelessness at his own weakness when he had been desperate to make amends for his earlier failure? Did he then become aware of the enormity of his denial and of the way he had tried to deceive himself as well as those in the courtyard? Not only was Peter shocked at how fickle he had been, but more than that, he was devastated that Jesus knew he had denied him, and at how deeply that had wounded him. He could do nothing but weep.

One of the things it is hard to convey to others are the times when we cannot express our feelings, when we are so overwhelmed that all we can do is sob, or shake, or rock with pain. However much we are asked "What is wrong?" we cannot find the words to express the depth of the despair or anger or agony. There may also be times when we cannot explain why we feel as we do or what has happened to trigger these feelings. We only know that the intense emotion erupting inside us is numbing us to everything else, even those we normally love and trust. No words can explain to those who have not experienced it, the despair, blackness, hatred and anger at ourselves or at others that chokes our breathing. There are times when there are no words, only tears.

There Are No Words

Peter: There are no words
        to express this pain
        only sobs
        ripped from my heart
        splitting my being
        stopping my breath
        and tearing my soul from within.

        My grief stops my breath
        but my tears do not stop
        they stream down my cheeks
        cascading,
        overflowing
        overwhelming
        everything else.

        My tears do not stop
        and neither does the agony
        there is no reassurance
        that can ease this flow
        no healing touch
        that can put this right.

        I want only to hide,
        until the tears no longer flow
        and the agony stops.

        Do not come near,
        you will not help.

God our Maker, you are here, holding us in our despair.

Jesus our Redeemer, you are here beside us,
understanding our wordless agony.

Spirit of Compassion, you are here within us,
breaking down the barriers to set free our pain.

We are God's People, held in our desolation by God's everlasting arms.

FRIDAY

a day of pain

17   Keeping Silent

> Now the chief priests and the whole council were looking for false testimony against Jesus so that they might put him to death, but they found none, though many false witnesses came forward. At last two came forward and said, "This fellow said, 'I am able to destroy the temple of God and to build it in three days.'" The high priest stood up and said, "Have you no answer? What is it that they testify against you?" But Jesus was silent.
>
> *Matthew 26:59-63a*

This is a puzzling incident. Why did Jesus say nothing in his defence? He could easily have explained what he had meant when he was talking about the destruction of the temple, so why did he say nothing? The answer that he was keeping silent because he knew that he had to die is too simplistic, too fatalistic and ignores the basic human instinct to stay alive with which Jesus wrestled in Gethsemane. I think his silence was more to do with the frustration of knowing that no one is really listening, so it is simpler to say nothing at all.

Feeling that no one is really listening is a common experience when mental health issues are involved. Conclusions are reached without consultation, and judgement given on behaviour or attitudes that we have not been able to defend as if we have no capacity to make decisions for ourselves. We can try to give an explanation, to help people understand, but everything we or anyone else says about us is dismissed or twisted to another meaning. It's like being told, "I'm sick of listening to your lies" when you have never been given the opportunity to speak, to explain, never mind tell lies. So it is simpler to maintain our integrity by saying nothing and not give our detractors more opportunity to hurt us.

Jesus, You Were Silent

Jesus,
you were silent
when you could have spoken,
spoken to save your life,
corrected their misunderstanding
or shouted your innocence,
protested at the injustice,
revealed their deceit.

But you were silent.
And in your silence
I hear the silence of the
oppressed
who dare not speak,
who cannot speak
even in their own defence.

In your silence
I hear the bewildered silence
of those to whom we will not listen
because their story
is difficult for us to hear.
It brings trouble,
makes us uncomfortable,
reveals our inadequacies,
uncovers our weakness.
So we shout our story
until they are silenced,
bewildered, shocked, shattered,
that no one will listen.

In your silence
I hear the terrified silence
of the victims of abuse.
Too afraid to speak out

petrified of the next assault,
they are silent
and endure the suffering,
gagged by humiliation and shame.

In your silence
I hear the enforced silence
of oppressive regimes
where thought is dangerous
and speech is worse
and people of faith
are terrorised into silence.

In your silence
I hear the hurt, angry silence
of those who dare not speak
because their words are not heard
their meaning is twisted
to suit someone else's purpose
to build a case against them
rather than to understand
and care for them.

Jesus,
you were silent
when you could have spoken.
You could have pushed back your darkness
changed your future
but if you had spoken
you would not have changed the world,
you would not have understood
the suffering silence
of the bewildered, the abused,
the oppressed, the misunderstood.

In your silence,
you stand with them.

God our Maker, you are here,
forgiving us for not listening, for jumping to conclusions.

Jesus our Redeemer, you are here beside us,
understanding why we remain silent and why it hurts when no one
listens.

Spirit of Truth, you are here within us,
helping us to maintain our integrity and speak the truth.

We are God's People, held in our frustrations and heard in our silence.

18   When We Cannot Get Answers

> Now Jesus stood before the governor; and the governor asked him, "Are you the King of the Jews?" Jesus said, "You say so." But when he was accused by the chief priests and elders, he did not answer. Then Pilate said to him, "Do you not hear how many accusations they make against you?" But he gave him no answer, not even to a single charge, so that the governor was greatly amazed.
>
> *Matthew 27: 11-14*

How did Pilate feel when Jesus refused to speak to him? He had the power to listen to Jesus' side of the story and even change his future. He may have been wondering who Jesus was protecting by his silence and why Jesus would take the blame for something he had not done. It was a course of action that he could not understand, so he was confused and may have been thinking, 'If you will not speak, how can I help you?' As Jesus maintained his silence and refused to take the opportunity to deny the charges and prove his innocence, Pilate's amazement could easily have turned to frustration and anger so that in washing his hands of Jesus he was demonstrating that he would not take responsibility for something for which Jesus would not take responsibility himself.

When seen in this light, this incident can resonate with the helplessness we feel when we are trying to help someone who will not reach out themselves and take the help that is offered. Pilate had the power to change or even dismiss the charges against Jesus, but Jesus did not grasp the opportunity he was offered. There are times when, however much we offer to help, people simply say nothing, or change the subject. Their body language tells us that there is something wrong but they deny it. Yet we cannot force out of them what is upsetting them. It is frustrating and can be hurtful. It is not easy for us to understand why offers of help are declined, so we feel snubbed or unworthy of their trust and our feelings of rejection can cloud our judgement of how to act next. We may be tempted to do as Pilate did, wash our hands of the whole mess and give up on the person in need.   But we do not know what is happening inside their head, or what has happened to destroy their ability to trust others and seal their lips with fear.

Why Should You Be Different?

To Pilate: You offer to listen
to hear my story
to ease my pain
to help.

But why should I trust you?
I've seen this before,
I've tried it before
and no one listened.
They did not even hear my words
except to scoff
and twist my meaning.

Why should you be different
from those who have taunted,
and teased,
pushed me around,
and trampled my dignity?

You lean forward, earnestly
imploring me to speak
frustrated by my silence
wanting to fix my problems
with a quick solution.
But there is no quick fix
no easy way out.
The only way,
is to face the pain.
And I do not trust you
your impatience
your desire for a solution
makes me shrink away

and raise my barriers.

So I cannot speak
I will not speak
because you are no different
from everyone else.

I do not want to place my trust
into hands
so eager to pass it on
and wash it away
feeling satisfied with a job well done.

God our Maker, you are here,
forgiving us for wanting a quick solution,
for judging too quickly,
and for not really listening to what is wrong.

Jesus our Redeemer, you are here beside us,
understanding why we let the pain wash over us without touching us
for fear of being unable to cope with it.

Spirit of Compassion, you are here within us,
helping us to find the strength to listen
and the courage to take on the real issues.

We are God's People, held in God's hands and heard in our pain.

19   When Someone Else Takes Our Place

Now at the festival the governor was accustomed to release a prisoner for the crowd, anyone whom they wanted. At that time they had a notorious prisoner, called Jesus Barabbas. So after they had gathered, Pilate said to them, "Whom do you want me to release for you, Jesus Barabbas or Jesus who is called the Messiah?" For he realized that it was out of jealousy that they had handed him over.

Matthew 27: 15-18

Many meditations on this passage focus on Barabbas' relief at escaping death or wonder why Jesus deserved to die in his place. This assumes that Barabbas was pleased to be released. Some commentators have suggested that he was a terrorist, fighting for the freedom of Israel, determined to drive out the Romans. If that was the case then it is possible that he resented being set free and therefore denied the opportunity to become a martyr for the cause in which he believed so passionately. He was 'saved' by others who made a decision that affected his life without consulting him.

This is often the experience of people with mental health issues, especially those whose mental capacity is believed to be impaired, such as those with dementia. Well-meaning friends take over tasks of which they are still capable, and make decisions for or about them, leaving those whom they are trying to help feeling frustrated, hurt and useless. They see someone else "in their place", fulfilling their roles and question why they are no longer wanted, or what they have done wrong. Instead of the expected gratitude they feel anger and resentment.

He Died In My Place
Barabbas: I was there,
                  waiting,
                  waiting in the darkness,
                  waiting to be led out to glory,
                  waiting to die for the cause,

waiting for my name to echo
through eternity.

I climbed up the steps
drinking in the roar of the crowd.
I squared my shoulders,
held my head high
ready to hear my name
shouted with pride
and with defiance,
ready to show my friends
that I was a man of my word.
I was ready
to do what I had set out to do,
what I had promised to do.

So when my name was shouted
not just by friends,
but by the whole crowd,
my heart swelled,
and I set my mind to dignity.

It was only when I saw him
being dragged away
and flogged
and mocked
whilst I was surrounded by jubilant friends
that the truth began to sink in.

He was in my place,
he was standing with my dignity,
taking my glory,
fulfilling my role,
taking responsibility
for what I had done.

He was in front of the crowds

whilst I was being dragged away,
hidden from view
as though my friends were ashamed of me.

My friends rejoiced,
shouting and clapping with joy,
congratulating themselves
because they had 'rescued' me
from my 'disgrace'.

They expected me to thank them
for treating me like a child
unable to make a choice
indulged and protected
from my own foolishness.

They told me
I should be thankful
that I was spared,
that I am free,
but I feel only grief
and despair.
This was my responsibility
my hour of glory
my chance to show my worth,
my chance to speak out
to share my story
and I have been silenced
and denied.
My place has been wrenched from me.

I am angry,
hurt,
bewildered
that people do not understand
why I do not rejoice
at being replaced.

How can I rejoice at freedom
when it gags my voice
and binds my hands?

I stand and stare
as he is whipped,
as he carries my cross,
as he stumbles to his death.
HE is in MY place.
HIS name will be
        remembered
not mine.
I stand and stare
seeing myself there
in my place.

God our Maker, you are here,
forgiving us for pushing others aside
and thinking that we are being helpful.

Jesus our Saviour, you are here beside us,
understanding why we want to take over from those who struggle,
and the weight of the burden of responsibility.

Spirit of God, you are here within us,
helping us to step back,
to trust others and not interfere.

We are God's People, called to love one another,
with all our imperfections and struggles.

20   When No One Is On Our Side

> Now the chief priests and the elders persuaded the crowds to ask for Barabbas and to have Jesus killed. The governor again said to them, "Which of the two do you want me to release for you?" And they said, "Barabbas." Pilate said to them, "Then what should I do with Jesus who is called the Messiah?" All of them said, "Let him be crucified!"
>
> *Matthew 27: 20-22*

Pilate tried to find ways to release Jesus, even declaring him innocent, but the religious leaders needed to get rid of him because he was upsetting the settled order of things. Pilate suggested an amnesty whereby Jesus could be set free, "as was the custom". This did not suit the chief priests and elders, so they persuaded the crowds to ask for Barabbas and to have Jesus killed. We are not told how they achieved this, whether it was with bribery or with threats of future persecution. Another suggestion made is that the crowd shouted for Barabbas because they did not want to be cheated of their rights. The custom was to release someone who was genuinely guilty, not someone they knew to be innocent, so they shouted for Barabbas. However it was done, they achieved their aim and the crowd shouted for Barabbas and condemned Jesus to crucifixion.

When we condense the events of Easter into a week, it is hard for us to understand how the people who cheered Jesus into Jerusalem on Sunday could have turned against him by the following Friday morning. It is possible that they were carried along by the tide of events on both occasions, that they simply joined in with what was going on. And if it is bemusing for us now, how much more bewildering was it for the disciples as they witnessed it first hand. It is not inconceivable that there were faces amongst the crowd shouting for Barabbas who had seen Jesus overturn the tables in the temple, or who had listened to him as he taught in the temple courts, or who witnessed his healing miracles. The disciples could well have stared at them in horror and tried to persuade them to change their minds. The voices of the crowd remind us how easily we can be swept up in a tide of emotion so that we find ourselves agreeing with opinions we do not hold.

There are other voices in the crowd, those of the disciples and members of Jesus' family, who were shouting frantically for Barabbas, and who were shouted down by their neighbours, whose voices were not heard in the clamour started by Jesus' opponents in the name of expediency. Supporting people who have periods when they are unable to care for themselves can feel the same, when letters requesting help from Social Services are ignored, or health workers do not listen to symptoms, preferring their own preformed diagnosis and solution. It feels as if the voice of truth is drowned by the voices of budgets, workload or criticism. No one is listening to the people who matter, who are dealing with the problem daily and fighting for help with the best interests of the sufferer at heart.

Our Voices Were Not Heard
The Disciples: We tried to shout in your defence
    we had marshalled our arguments
    got our proof of your innocence
    but no one would listen
    no one wanted to know
    and the louder we shouted
    the more deaf the authorities became.

    Our voices were not heard
    we did not matter
    we were not important enough to matter.
    The authorities had made up their minds.
    You had to go.

    Our voices were not heard
    by those who thought their own importance
    was more important than us,
    but did you hear us,
    amidst the commotion

screaming your name
protesting your innocence
fighting your cause?

Did our voices penetrate
the cacophony of hate
of prejudice
of lies
to support you
and enfold you?

We tried,
we tried so hard
we believed in you
we still believe in you
but our voices were not heard.

God our Maker, you are here,
forgiving us for being carried along by the crowd
or for ignoring the voices that shout inconvenient truths.

Jesus our Redeemer, you are here beside us,
understanding our frustration when we are not heard
and our despair when a tide of emotion washes over others.

Spirit of Strength, you are here within us,
helping us to hold fast to the truth, even when others deny it.

We are God's People, called to shout for truth, justice and love.

21   When We Feel Helpless To Help

> So Pilate released Barabbas for them; and after flogging Jesus, he handed him over to be crucified. Then the soldiers of the governor took Jesus into the governor's headquarters, and they gathered the whole cohort around him. They stripped him and put a scarlet robe on him, and after twisting some thorns into a crown, they put it on his head. They put a reed in his right hand and knelt before him and mocked him, saying, "Hail, King of the Jews!" They spat on him, and took the reed and struck him on the head. After mocking him, they stripped him of the robe and put his own clothes on him. Then they led him away to crucify him.
>
> *Matthew 27: 26-31*

Matthew's words conjure up a scene that is horribly familiar and deeply uncomfortable. What he describes is the bullying of an individual by a crowd because he is different, and the victim's isolation when no one steps in to help. The soldiers enjoy his humiliation because they believe he deserves it for daring to challenge the familiar order and feel justified in their inhumanity because they believe he is worthless. Sadly, this still happens today when people who are judged to be "outsiders" or "different" are set upon, teased, bullied and made to feel worthless because they are of a different faith, mental capacity, skin tone or even simply supporters of a rival football team. In the worst cases they are left with life-changing injuries. As we are reminded of Jesus' isolation and suffering, we are challenged to think about whether we are prepared to defend the defenceless, whether with words or action, to prevent further suffering.

However, that is not the perspective from which the meditation is written. It tries to imagine the thoughts of the disciples who shouted for Jesus to be released and were not heard. After watching Barabbas walk free, they had to watch Jesus being scourged and mocked and must have been seething with anger and frustration that they were powerless to help. Amidst the jeering of the crowd and the fervour of the soldiers, they would have been afraid of reprisal, or of making things worse by intervening and angering the authorities further. Would they have stayed and watched the whipping and the mocking, screaming that it should stop, or would they have walked away? There is no evidence that any of the disciples watched Jesus being flogged, but the detailed gospel accounts suggest that at least some of them were there and later told the others what had happened.

This brings to mind those who come alongside people struggling with difficult situations, whether that is a mental health issue, a cancer diagnosis, the end of a relationship, bereavement or redundancy. It can be at these times that we feel tongue-tied and awkward because we don't know what to say or do for the best, and the person struggling feels isolated and misunderstood. Yet if we do try to speak or act, we know that we are in danger of making the situation worse rather than better. So all we can do is sit in the pain and struggle and feel every hurt they experience. And that is the frustration the disciples must have felt, knowing that there was nothing they could do except watch and pray, and console Jesus with their presence.

For many people, their first reaction when confronted with a difficult situation is to think "what can I do to help?" so that they can busy themselves with practicalities rather than doing nothing. Matthew was chosen as the narrator for this meditation because, as a former tax collector, he could have had contacts and perhaps influence with the Romans, and been desperate to use it to save Jesus from the pain, and felt so impotent when he realised it was hopeless to try.

I Couldn't Do Anything
Matthew: I stood and watched
as they whipped him.
I felt every lash,
heard every silent scream
and echoed them with my own.
I tensed every muscle
as the whip whistled through the air,

and winced with every blow
that cracked into his flesh.

I wished I could look away,
walk away,
not see his anguish
or his vulnerability
as he was tormented and taunted
by faceless, nameless officials.

But I couldn't walk away
I couldn't turn from a friend in need.
I hoped he knew I was there,
praying for him,
giving him my strength
as his ebbed away.

I was desperate to help.
I wanted to take the blows
to give him a break.
But there was a ring of lances
and indifferent Roman soldiers
between him and me.

I looked at the soldiers.
They were men I had known
when I collected taxes
and handed them over to officials
in their protective presence.
I scanned their ranks
anxious, frantic,
to find someone I knew.

But my stomach turned
looking at known, friendly faces,
twisted now beyond recognition
grotesquely distorted by bloodlust

and enjoyment of torture
of a man they do not know.

Pleasant voices,
hoarse with cheering
each echoing lash.
Some clapped
as each stroke
drove deeper into his flesh.

I could not look here
for compassion and mercy
even in people I thought I knew.
Their hearts were hardened by prejudice
and they were blinded
to truth and justice
by expedience
and the need to follow others.

I was desperate
to stop this madness
this insanity of torture,
but I couldn't.
So instead I screamed inside:
"Why
  have they come to believe that you deserve this?
  How
  can your loving Father stand by doing nothing?
  Where
  are the miracles that healed and helped others?
  Why
  can I do nothing to help?"

He didn't answer,
no one answered,
no one reached out
as he fell to the ground.

God our Maker, you are here,
holding us in our frustration
when we are desperate to help
and there is nothing we can do.

Jesus our Redeemer, you are here beside us,
understanding why we are desperate for answers
when everything seems impossible.

Spirit of Compassion, you are here within us,
encouraging us to stay alongside those who are suffering
and support them with our presence.

We are God's People, held in the love of God,
giving strength to those in need.

22   When We Are Compelled To Help

> As they led him away, they seized a man, Simon of Cyrene, who was coming from the country, and they laid the cross on him, and made him carry it behind Jesus.
>
> *Luke 23:26*

Simon of Cyrene has become a symbol of those who are willing to share the burdens of others, even in the most difficult circumstances. Yet according to Luke he did not volunteer to carry Jesus' cross; he was made to carry it by the soldiers. Luke does not say why the decision was made for someone else to carry Jesus' cross, but it is easy to imagine Jesus' exhaustion after a sleepless night and a day of interrogation and trial, and how that would make him slow and stumbling in his walk. The authorities would have impressed on the soldiers the need to hurry because the Sabbath was approaching meaning that Jesus needed to be crucified before sunset when the holy day started. So a man was drawn into the confusion for no other reason that that he happened to be in that place at that time.

This can happen so easily, that we are drawn into the pain or struggle of someone else by circumstance, such as witnessing a crime or an accident and going to help, or being the next door neighbour of someone who needs care, or by ties of family being drawn into a caring role that we do not want. We become unwilling confidantes of secrets we would rather not know and feel unable to walk away in case the person for whom we are caring is unable to cope. The care we offer is not given freely and generously, but grudgingly, resenting the time and energy it takes. Simon of Cyrene, who carried the burden of the cross, felt the weight of responsibility on his shoulders for someone he had never met. His voice speaks of unwilling compassion and feeling unable to walk away.

I Had No Choice

Simon: I was dragged into this mess against my will.
I was just a bystander.
I'd never met this man before,
heard of him,
but I was not that interested.
I'd come up to Jerusalem for the festival,
was trying to get through the narrow streets,
trying to get on with my business
when I was caught up in a crowd
following the criminals on their way to execution,
staggering under the weight of their crosses.

I was pulled from the anonymity of the crowd
as strong arms grabbed mine
and pushed me alongside
one of the men,
who had stumbled to a stop.
"Help him."
"Take the weight for him."
I was surprised at their compassion
helping this broken, bleeding man,
until I realised that with approaching nightfall
they were not driven by compassion,
but expediency.

I looked for a way out
but was hemmed in by officials.
I didn't want to be associated with him.
I didn't want to be contaminated
by his trouble
or by his blood.

But I had no choice,
I knelt beside the man,
took the weight of the crossbar,
and started to walk alongside him.

He didn't speak,
I don't think he had the energy.
And if he had,
I wouldn't have listened.
I didn't want to know about his troubles
I had enough of my own.

As I followed him
I had to stop myself from wondering
what had brought him to this,
why he was so exhausted,
what he had done,
why he was being crucified.

I kept my eyes on the road,
stepping carefully
so that I didn't fall into him.
I was desperate for this to be over,
for him to be out of my life,
as desperate as he was
for it not to have come to this.
The road was never-ending,
narrows walls to negotiate
rocks to avoid,
unexpected twists and turns,
taking me farther from where I wanted to be
and further into his mess.

I wanted only to throw off this burden,
to walk away
and back to my ordinary life.
Yet when the weight was taken from me,
and nailed to his body,
I found I couldn't turn my back.
I watched as he was lifted up
and stayed to the bitter end
unable to tear myself away.

121

God our Maker, you are here,
forgiving us for being reluctant to help others and putting ourselves
first.

Jesus our Redeemer, you are here beside us,
understanding why we turn away from pain and responsibility.

Spirit of Compassion, you are here within us,
moving us to help others, despite ourselves.

We are God's People, given strength to bear one another's burdens
by the one who knows what it is to be overburdened.

23   When Our Experience Helps Others

> Two others also, who were criminals, were led away to be put to death with him. When they came to the place that is called The Skull, they crucified Jesus there with the criminals, one on his right and one on his left. Then Jesus said, "Father, forgive them; for they do not know what they are doing."
>
> *Luke 23: 32-34a*

It can be hard to acknowledge that people who are suffering have something to offer. We know that when we are struggling we can feel so overwhelmed by the illness, injury or grief that we cannot cope with the thought of someone's pain. We close our eyes and ears to them, finding it hard to accept that they might have something to offer. Caring for others whilst we are in pain does not fit with the way we are taught that the world is organised. In that world-view, the unwell are nursed by the well, the elderly are cared for by younger generations, and bad experiences should be consigned to the past as they cannot help others.

Yet as Jesus hung on the cross he continued to minister, despite incredible pain. He offered consolation to his mother, compassion to the criminals crucified with him, and forgiveness to those who had brought him to this place and nailed him to the cross. His voice of loving care speaks to us and reassures us that our experiences can help others, can help us to understand and give meaning to our suffering, if we are prepared to share our pain.

Even As You Suffered, You Ministered

> Jesus,
> you continued to care
> even through unimaginable pain
> and searing grief.
> How could you do it?
> When I am overwhelmed,
> by the anger and hurt

of betrayal by friends
and denial by those I am asked to trust,
I lack the love to reach out
or the strength to care.

When I am drowning in pain
when I feel abandoned and rejected
by those in authority
who have rejected me
just as Pilate washed his hands of you,
who choose not to temper justice with mercy
or legislation with compassion,
I have no energy to think of others
or desire to hear another's pain.

Yet,
as physical pain ripped through your body
and racked your being with agony,
you were still able to look at others
and recognise their need
and respond with love and compassion
offering hope in despair
and comfort in desolation.

Was it your love for them
that gave you the strength
to overcome your own pain?
Was it your understanding of their need
that gave you the energy
to reach out?

Lord,
in my pain,
give me that strength of love
and understanding
so that in my grief
I can reach out to the grief of others.

God our Maker, you are here,
forgiving us for hiding from pain,
and assuming those we help have nothing to offer.

Jesus our Redeemer, you are here beside us,
understanding why we need to reach out,
and why we hide from pain.

Spirit of God, you are here within us,
helping us to listen and learn from others,
and find meaning in our suffering.

We are God's People, held in Christ's love-scarred hands.

24　Anguish For A Child

Meanwhile, standing near the cross of Jesus were his mother, and his mother's sister, Mary the wife of Clopas, and Mary Magdalene. When Jesus saw his mother and the disciple whom he loved standing beside her, he said to his mother, "Woman, here is your son." Then he said to the disciple, "Here is your mother." And from that hour the disciple took her into his own home.

John 19: 25b-27

Mary's anguish as she helplessly watched her son suffering is poignant and heart-rending. With the force of a mother's love she would have done anything to save Jesus from that pain, would willingly have taken his place, but all she could do was to stand and suffer with him. What questions ran through her mind? What could her sister and the other Marys say to Jesus' mother that could possibly have comforted her? Jesus reached out to her and offered a substitute 'son' for whom she can care, but it is hard to imagine that anyone could have taken the place of her first born for whom she endured so much at the time of his birth.

As we hear Mary's voice of intense grief, it touches a chord in many ways with many people. Those who walk alongside people with mental health issues can find echoes of their experiences in Mary's wretchedness, in particular her struggle to understand what has led her son to this moment, her desperation to help and her frustration that there is nothing she can do. Mary at the foot of the cross, helplessly watching her son suffer also resonates with those who have nursed loved ones through illness, alleviating pain, encouraging, comforting, grieving and listening, As they kept their final vigil at the bedside they knew the helplessness of caring when that there was nothing more they could do. Like Mary, they were powerless to do anything other than watch and wait. Her anguish also touches the hearts of those who have been suddenly bereaved as they wrestle with the questions of "why" and "if only" that inevitably follow. However, the passage does not end with Mary's grief but with Jesus' compassion for her and his beloved disciple. In this he demonstrates that he understands the depth of our pain as it tears us apart and encourages us to find strength in the company of those who share our experiences, so that we can support one another.

How Did This Happen?

Mary: What has happened to you, my son?
I brought you into the world,
took you to safety
when you were threatened,
eased your pain when you fell
and soothed your nightmares
with gentleness and love.

I encouraged you in your dreams,
prompted you to fulfil your vocation,
travelled with you
down every road,
supported you when others turned away,
argued for you
when our family disagreed with you
and wanted to disown you.

And now I am watching you die,
hearing your cries
knowing that I cannot reach you,
that a mother's touch
is no longer enough
to ease this waking nightmare.

I can no longer cradle you
to take away your hurt
or soothe your pain.
I can only watch
as you struggle for breath
and life ebbs away.

Where did I go wrong?
When did I fail to understand you?
I did not understand
how much you were hurting
and why you needed to die
to make things right.
There must be another way,
please God, let there be another way.

You have offered me another son,
as if you are replaceable,
but I love the son I have.
I do not always agree with you
I do not always praise you
I have not always understood you
but you are my son,
my beloved son,
and I must cradle you
one last time
in death.

God our Maker, you are here,
holding us in our anguish and grief.

Jesus our Redeemer, you are here beside us,
reaching out with compassion and offering us comfort.

Spirit of Strength, you are here within us,
helping us to face the difficult questions,
and to persist until we find the answers.

We are God's People, supporting one another in prayer and love.

25 Despair

> When Judas, his betrayer, saw that Jesus was condemned, he repented and brought back the thirty pieces of silver to the chief priests and the elders. He said, "I have sinned by betraying innocent blood." But they said, "What is that to us? See to it yourself." Throwing down the pieces of silver in the temple, he departed: and he went and hanged himself.
>
> *Matthew 27: 3-5*

Throughout history, Judas Iscariot's name has been synonymous with betrayal and double agency, yet this passage seems to show that he has been misrepresented. When the reality of what he had set in motion dawned on him, he wanted to undo it, as far as he could. The Chief Priests denied responsibility and refused to help him, wanting not to be contaminated by his sin. He felt so alone and so marked as a failure that he went out and hanged himself. Rather than exploring what brought him to such despair, this passage should prompt us to consider what, other than greed, could have motivated him to turn from being a follower to an enemy of Jesus. After all, he believed that Jesus was the one who could achieve freedom for Israel. Did he change his mind about Jesus or was he convinced by other revolutionaries that betraying Jesus was the way to provoke the uprising for which they longed? His story is a stark illustration to us of how easy it is for motives to be misunderstood and actions misinterpreted. It shows how quickly we can jump to conclusions about other people and how ready we are to believe the worst of others rather than looking for another explanation.

When things go wrong because of misunderstanding, it can lead to bitter regret and despair that we will ever be understood because we are not heard, or are labelled by previous actions, as Judas continues to be. Sadly, people with mental health problems are often pre-judged and their motivation ascribed to illness rather than being evaluated on an individual basis. They are condemned for being selfish, or shallow, or not worth considering because they are too much trouble, leaving them feeling that they have no intrinsic worth. In the same way, the Gospel writers ascribe meanness and selfishness to Judas without trying to understand his character. When things go wrong because we have misunderstood, or have been misunderstood, it is incredibly hard to explain ourselves without being accused of making up excuses for bad behaviour. Alternatively, we can be rebuffed, as Judas was by the High Priests, because people do not understand that our regret is real and our need for forgiveness is great. And, as Judas discovered, the hardest person to forgive for the mistake is ourselves. It is at that point that we need to understand that we are all human, that we all get things wrong, and that forgiveness is always possible.

It Wasn't Supposed To Be Like This
Judas: It wasn't supposed to be like this
I didn't want his destruction
I wanted a revolution.
The kiss wasn't supposed to be the beginning of the end
it was supposed to be the beginning of the new life
of Jesus' new Kingdom.
I was trying to trap the soldiers,
not Jesus.
I lured them to a place
where we could overwhelm them
and leave the authorities unprotected.

For one brief moment
when someone lashed out
and cut off a man's ear,
I thought it had started,
that we were going to claim a glorious victory.
But Jesus stopped us,
sent us away
as he went away
to his trial.

It wasn't supposed to be like this.
Jesus wasn't supposed to be on trial.
It was supposed to be the authorities on trial,
the Pharisees, the Romans
on trial for oppressing us
with rules, regulations and taxes.
Where was your fight, Jesus?
You were supposed to fight back
to uncover the authorities' collusion
with wealth and oppression.
But you stayed silent
and let them oppress you.

It wasn't supposed to be like this
with Jesus, the leader,
whipped and mocked.
He was supposed to lead the whipping
of those who abuse God's grace
just as he whipped the traders in the temple.
Why did you stop there Jesus?
Where did your anger go?
Why did you lose your passion for God's truth?

It wasn't supposed to be like this
Jesus staggering under the weight of the cross,
defeated,
bruised,
bleeding,
shamed,
battered by insults,
blinded by tears and blood.

What has blinded you to the possibilities, Jesus,
the possibilities of change
and freedom from oppression?

Why did you not take the opportunity
to encourage others,
to lead others
to your glorious Kingdom?

It wasn't supposed to be like this,
Jesus, hanging on a cross,
like a common criminal,
broken,
destroyed,
his disciples in shock
despairing,
bewildered,
broken by grief
torn apart by his cries.

I wanted to reach out to Peter,
to Andrew, to James, to John,
to explain why I had done it,
to share in their grief
to be included,
and welcomed.
But I am afraid
and ashamed to show my face.
I don't think they understand.

Do I understand?
Have I misunderstood?
Was he not ready?
Was it not true?

He preached revolution,
I gave my life to him
took risks for him
had dealings with the enemy for him
lost friends because of him.

I'm now alone,
deserted by both sides
because of him.

Have I misunderstood?
Have I destroyed him?
Have I ruined everything?
His final, dying scream echoes round my skull.
"My God, my God, why have you forsaken me?"

Did I make him lose his faith
his unbreakable,
unshakeable faith
in his Father God?
O God,

I have destroyed him,
our best hope,
our last hope
our only hope.
It's over.
Hope is destroyed with him.

There's nothing left.
What have I done?

God our Maker, you are here,
forgiving us for misunderstanding others
and for jumping to conclusions without listening.

Jesus our Redeemer, you are here beside us,
understanding why we fall into despair,
and lose hope that we will ever be understood.

Spirit of Compassion, you are here within us,
helping us to forgive ourselves, and others,
when we fall into despair.

We are God's People, held forever in his arms, and there is nowhere
that is too dark or distant for him to reach us.

26   When We Feel Abandoned

> From noon on, darkness came over the whole land until three in the afternoon. And about three o'clock Jesus cried with a loud voice, "Eli, Eli, lema sabachthani?" that is, "My God, my God, why have you forsaken me?"
>
> Then Jesus cried again with a loud voice and breathed his last.
>
> *Matthew 27: 45, 46, 50*

The final words of Jesus as reported by Matthew are known as the 'Cry of Dereliction', and it is easy to see why. His anguished cry to God for understanding and comfort reveal so much about his feelings of desolation and abandonment. Jesus chose to use the opening verse of Psalm 22 which continues, "why are you so far from saving me, so far from my cries of anguish?" He was desperate to know that there was a purpose in what was happening, and yet his pleas to God seemed to be unanswered.

This feeling of desolation and abandonment, underpinned by an urgent longing to know that God is not absent, is something that we all experience at difficult times in our lives. We can be plagued with questions, guilt and doubt about why God does not answer, blaming ourselves for not having enough faith, or not being worthy of God's attention. Yet in this passage we see that even Jesus felt this despair, this abandonment, this dereliction. Instead of being strong in faith to encourage others, this passage reveals Jesus' despair and vulnerability. This helps us to see that faith can survive feelings of abandonment, fear and despair, and that through his anguish and doubt on the cross, Jesus is with us in our darkness and despair.

But there is more to this than realising that Jesus is with us in our despair, there is also the awareness that we can minister to others in times of our own doubt and uncertainty. Jesus on the cross was not afraid to be vulnerable, was not afraid to show his anguish and struggle.

Too often people who are struggling are seen as the recipients of care rather than the givers, those who need comfort rather than being able to offer it from a place of empathy. Being unafraid to share our times of vulnerability can be a very powerful way of witnessing to our faith that God has not and will not let us go.

Where Are You, God?

Jesus,
you also knew desolation,
your cry of dereliction,
searching for God
screaming at God
for being absent,
for being silent,
tears at our hearts
and reveals your agony,
your vulnerability,
your humanity,
and your capacity
to understand our pain.

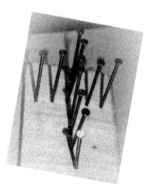

Through your pain
your agony,
your desolation,
you inspire us
to be vulnerable
to share our pain
to reveal our fallibility
and our humanity
to bring strength
and hope to others.
Through your scream of desertion
you encourage us,
to scream at God,
to demand answers
to impossible questions.

Through your pain
you are with us in ours,
and we know
that, like you,
we will not be overcome.

God our Maker, you are here,
forgiving us for doubting and despairing.

Jesus our Redeemer, you are here beside us,
screaming with us in our agony, holding us in our desolation
and inspiring us to have the courage to be vulnerable.

Spirit of Perseverance, you are here within us,
helping us to endure God's silence.
We are God's People, whom God never abandons.

27   When It Feels Like The End

> Then Jesus, crying with a loud voice, said, "Father, into your hands I commend my spirit." Having said this, he breathed his last. When the centurion saw what had taken place, he praised God and said, "Certainly this man was innocent." And when all the crowds who had gathered there for this spectacle saw what had taken place, they returned home, beating their breasts. But all his acquaintances, including the women who had followed him from Galilee, stood at a distance, watching these things.
>
> It was the day of Preparation, and the Sabbath was beginning.   The women who had come with him from Galilee followed [when Jesus' body was taken from the cross], and they saw the tomb and how his body was laid.   Then they returned, and prepared spices and ointments.
>
> *Luke 23:46-49, 56*

In Luke's account Jesus' final words are not as desolate as Matthew's, but they are as final. It is clear that everything is over, there will be no sudden miraculous intervention. Jesus' life has ended, and with it the hopes of his disciples and followers come crashing down. Luke says that the crowds returned home, beating their breasts, but his acquaintances continued to watch. The disciples must have felt a great deal of uncertainty about the future so it is understandable that they lingered, not wanting to let go of their leader, wondering, "is this it?" and questioning why there was nothing more they could do or say, and utterly uncertain about what to do next.

It is a situation to which it is easy to relate. It is hard to walk away from a momentous event, whether it is a celebration or a time of mourning, without a feeling of loss and finality. There is a temptation to remain where we are, to stay "in the moment", however painful that may be, so that we do not need to return to ordinary life and admit that this particular period of our lives is over. We may be left wondering "Is this it? Is it actually over?" as if we had expected more or feel cheated that the time has been so short. We are reluctant to move on, leave behind the experience and revisit it only through souvenirs and memories.

Sometimes mental health issues are perceived as an inability to move on from trauma or loss. Sufferers are encouraged to "stop dwelling on it" as if flashbacks are voluntary or "let go of it" as if they are stubbornly gripping painful memories in their hands like a toddler who does not want to be separated from a favourite toy. Staying in the moment is not a choice, but an ever-present nightmare. The question "is this it?" loses its connotation of the time being too short and becomes instead a desperate plea to discover that there is more to life than this imprisonment in trauma.

It is in this sense that Thomas asks the question, "Is this it?" as he stands in bewilderment at the foot of the cross. He is transfixed by the immense trauma of which he is a part and cannot imagine a time when he will be able to leave it behind, and is struggling to make sense of what he has seen.

Is This It?
Thomas: Is this it?
                Is this the end he has proclaimed?
                Has he really gone?
                Even seeing his blood flow
                down his tortured body
                could not persuade me
                that he had died.

                I cannot believe that he has gone,
                that there will be no more wise words
                no more encouragement to love
                or invitations to hope.

                I wasn't with the others
                at the foot of the cross,
                but I too stood and watched
                as they drove in those nails,

140

each blow of the hammer
shuddering through me,
wrenching my heart
as they tore apart his flesh.

I stood apart from the others
as I watched him suffer,
the nails ripping holes in his hands
as he was lifted up,
exposed to ridicule
helpless
suffering
beyond my reach.

I was close enough to hear
his words of comfort
to his mother
to the others
to the thief at his side,
even asking forgiveness
for those who crucified him.

I was close enough to see
the grief on their faces,
the inconsolable, overwhelming grief
that stopped my heart from beating
that made it hard to breathe.

I wanted to cry out
"Why?"
"Why is this happening?"
"What has he done wrong?"
But I had no breath
other than strangled sobs
of despair.

In disbelief,
I heard the taunts
of religious leaders
of 'holy men'
"He claimed to save others
  but he cannot save himself."
congratulating each other
with cruel laughter
on a job well done.

I wanted to scream in anger,
"Look at what you've done
  a good man suffering agony
  because of your weakness
  your jealousy,
  your fear."

But I could not.
I could only stand and watch,
could only pray for a miracle
with no hope that it would come.

How could anyone recover
from such wounds?
Even Jesus
with his healing powers
could not save himself.

The hope died
with his final cry
"It is finished"
And the spear was plunged
deep into his side.

I feel numb
nothing left
nothing to give

I cannot speak
I do not want to meet anyone
I want only to lock the door
and be alone.

Most of all,
I want to know, Jesus,
what next?
What do you want us to do?

Or is this it?
Is it finished?
For him, for me,
for everyone.
It is finished.

God our Maker, you are here,
forgiving us for being unable to move on to new things.

Jesus our Redeemer, you are here beside us,
understanding when we fail to grasp what is happening,
when all we want is to turn back the clock and try again.

Spirit of Compassion, you are here within us,
helping us to console one another,
and find meaning where there seems to be only confusion.

We are God's People, held in our uncertainty
by our vulnerable, loving God.

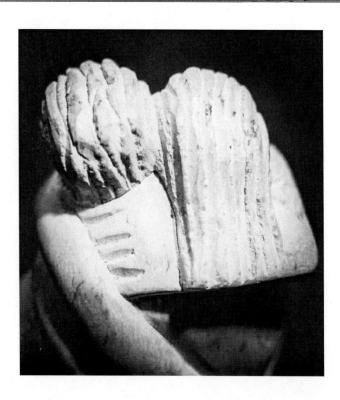

28 Embracing Uncertainty

Then Jesus cried again with a loud voice and breathed his last. At that moment the curtain of the temple was torn in two, from top to bottom. The earth shook, and the rocks were split.

Matthew 27:50-51

In these two verses, Matthew turns the focus away from Golgotha and alludes to the earth-shattering events elsewhere in Jerusalem. As Jesus died, the curtain in the Temple was torn in two, revealing the Holy of Holies previously only entered by the High Priest. The inclusion of the tearing of the curtain seems almost an afterthought, a sideshow to the important events at the crucifixion, yet it shook the foundations of the worshipping community just as much as the earthquake shattered the rocks. The torn curtain demonstrated that God was no longer restricted by the walls of the Temple and that access to God was for everyone, not just the elite who knew the right way to speak and had the correct clothes to wear. The aftershocks of this event are still rocking the Church today as debates continue about who should be entitled to preside at worship, or to be ordained as leaders, and the appropriate dress and language for worship.

God breaking out of the Holy of Holies is not just a symbol for Good Friday, but a warning that we should never try to restrict God to our own need for certainty and perfection. God cannot be contained by our tidy rules or kept out of the untidiness of the world. God in the person of Jesus of Nazareth welcomed people with chaotic lives, with uncertain faith, with struggle and confusion. This means we do not need to be perfect to enter a place of worship, just aware that we are loved and cherished as we are. We now have to accept that we can bring our imperfections to worship and we do not need to leave them at the door. Sometimes our greatest witness is not what we do or how we are doing it but the fact that, despite our struggles, we still want to witness to God by doing it, however imperfect that witness might be. An encounter with God who embraces uncertainty is life-changing.

The Torn Curtain

The Faithful Priest:

I was still shaken by his anger
the violence
with which he confronted the traders,
the venom he spat at us
for allowing this to happen.
Maybe it was wrong to trade there,
but it was only the outermost court
for strangers and foreigners.
They would not know,
they would not understand,
that it was desecration.
They do not worship this God.
They are not good enough
to come through to this stillness,
this peace,
to God.

I did not go to the crucifixion,
I did not want to follow the mob.
He had upset the tables
and over-turned my world
but I did not need to see him destroyed.
I wanted only to feel the silence
kneeling before the altar
swathed in incense
watching the sacrifice
safe in ritual.

Without warning
the curtain was torn apart,
as if by unseen hands
and the silence was ripped
by the tearing of cloth.

Suddenly we could all see
right into the holiest place.
Light streaming in,
revealed the dust,
the drab emptiness,
but for a flickering lamp
diminished to almost nothing
by the intruding daylight.

What could it mean?
How had it happened?
Who had done it?

I looked around.
The few who were there
were terrified, shaken.
One or two were leaving,
hurrying off to find answers
or escape accusation.

I stared at the torn curtain,
created by our ancestors,
maintained for generations,
now in tatters on the floor.

I gazed at the empty sanctuary
created for God
kept apart for God
that God now seemed to have scorned.

Could this mean
that God cannot be contained
within buildings
within rituals
and vestments
careful rites and diction?

Is God above such human concern
for perfection
and repetition
that does not challenge us?

A life time's dedication
to observation
of rules and seasons
diet and dress
is now laid bare
and open to question.

Does this mean
that God is not contained
by the rules
we have knotted around our faith?
The shall nots,
must nots,
should nots,
can nots
that govern our every move?

Is this God
exploding into life
with can,
and why not,
trust, and try?

Then our faithful devotion
to rule and regulation
disguised as vocation
is brought to the light
and exposed to questions
of love and trust.

I looked again
at the dusty sanctuary,

the useless lamp,
the empty space,
and began to understand.

God breaks out of our barriers
and explodes into our lives
bringing chaos and doubt,
possibility and challenge,
reality and healing.

Now I see
that it does not matter what I wear
where I stand or how I stand.
It matters only that I stand
bearing witness to God
in the midst of chaos.

And if, in my fallibility,
I fumble for words
or in my frailty
I stumble, or forget where to turn,
it is not an offence
that should be condemned
by labelling me unworthy
inept, incompetent,
but a celebration of the God
who breaks down our barriers
and embraces all life -
weak and strong
faithful and unfaithful
ordinary and strange -
enveloping it with hope
and strengthening with understanding.

God our Maker, you are here,
forgiving us for striving for perfection
and for condemning those who do not achieve it.

Jesus our Redeemer, you are here beside us,
understanding why we surround ourselves with rules,
creating comfort in certainty and conformity.

Spirit of Life, you are here within us,
letting in the light of God's love
that embraces uncertainty and failure
and challenges us to do the same.

We are God's People, for whom there are no barriers between us and
the God who loves and treasures each one of us.

29   When What We Can Do Feels So Little

> When it was evening, there came a rich man from Arimathea, named Joseph, who was also a disciple of Jesus. He went to Pilate and asked for the body of Jesus; then Pilate ordered it to be given to him. So Joseph took the body and wrapped it in a clean linen cloth and laid it in his own new tomb, which he had hewn in the rock. He then rolled a great stone to the door of the tomb and went away.
>
> *Matthew 27: 57-60*

The only time that Joseph of Arimathea is mentioned in the Gospels is to recount how he approached Pilate for permission to bury Jesus' body. All that Matthew tells us is that he came from Arimathea and that he was wealthy, Mark includes the detail that he was a member of the Sanhedrin, and Luke adds that he had not participated in the conspiracy against Jesus because he did not agree with it. Joseph wanted to do something to help Jesus' grieving disciples and family, and found that all he could do was offer a tomb for which he had no use at the time.

When we are faced with a crisis, our natural response is to want to help. It is easiest when practical assistance is needed, but when those tasks are complete, we can feel helpless, wondering what else we can offer. Joseph of Arimathea offered a safe place for Jesus' body from where it could not be stolen or mutilated by his enemies. To Joseph it may not have seemed significant because the use of the tomb would not inconvenience him in any way, but it was something he could do, however small, in the face of other people's needs. For people who are struggling following a crisis of any sort, a safe space where worries can be aired or set aside is a haven that can bring strength. A smile or a quick message of solidarity conveys value and compassion that encourages them to persevere despite overwhelming obstacles. A phone call or an email may not seem much to those who are desperate to help, but they can be the seeds of resurrection to strugglers.

I Wanted To Do More

Joseph: I wanted to do more
I was desperate
to do something,
anything,
that would help
that would change things
and all I could do
was offer a cold place
unused and unneeded for now.

None of my riches
will secure his freedom
or bring him back to life.
All I could purchase
was privacy in my resting place
secure in its privileged seclusion,
a breathing space amidst the madness,
an oasis in the desert of despair.

None of my influence
could change the fact of his death
or the way he died.
All it won for him
was a safe place to rest
and dignity in death
away from the indignity
and anonymity
of the criminals' mass grave.

I wanted to do more
to change the past
to change the world
and all I could do
was offer something unneeded
that would not inconvenience me.

It felt cheap,
and not enough,
but there was nothing else.

It wasn't much,
but it brought sanctuary from worry
and spoke of love
in the face of distrust.
It wasn't much,
but it was enough.

God our Maker, you are here,
creating opportunities, however small,
for us to give what we can.

Jesus our Redeemer, you are here beside us,
understanding why we are moved to help,
and encouraging us to reach out in love.

Spirit of Compassion, you are here within us,
giving us courage to offer what we have,
whether it is everything or a little
to help others when they are confused and struggling.

We are God's People, bound together by love
and held in love-scarred hands.

SATURDAY

a day of endless waiting

30 Waiting

On the Sabbath they rested according to the commandment.

Luke 23: 56

The agony of 36 hours summed up in an unemotional half verse in Luke's Gospel. It seems almost an afterthought. Do we ever stop to think what the followers of Jesus must have gone through during that time? Their leader arrested, tried and put to death so quickly there was no time to organise resistance; grief for someone they had loved; grief for their loss of hope; grief over their lack of action for him; disturbed by Judas's betrayal and suicide? Luke says "they rested according to the commandment." It is hard to imagine them resting, paying attention to prayer when so much had happened. The Gospels suggest that they were together because that is how they were found by the women on Easter morning. If they were together, it is hard to see how they could wait together patiently, prayerfully, hopefully, without falling into discussion and accusation, because they were in such great agitation.

Like the disciples, at some point we have all experienced the agony of waiting, for academic exam results; for the outcome of medical tests; for the return home of a loved one; for legal procedures to run their course. So we do have some idea of how the disciples may have felt on that Sabbath, forced to inaction by Jewish Law. The problem is that we know the end of the story, so however much we enter into the emotions of Good Friday, we know that Easter Day will bring good news meaning that we tend to overlook this period of waiting. Yet it is a vital part of the story because it speaks to us of our own feelings of impotence in the face of other authorities, and of loss, bewilderment and grief when things take an unexpected turn. That was the starting point for this meditation.

Waiting, Waiting

James: Today is the Sabbath, the day of rest,
but how can we rest
with our minds running over so many things
but mostly,
why?
and how?

Why did this happen?
How did it go so wrong?
Why did it we let it go so far?
What could we have done
what should we have done
to stop it, to help?

We need answers,
but we have only questions
racing through our minds
pressing on our hearts,
pushing us together to talk
and forcing us apart as we disagree
and blame each other
for letting him down.

Yes, we scattered in fear from the garden,
running for our lives
but gradually we were drawn back together.
We were all there in small groups
as he died
in agony.

John was there,
wouldn't move,
until he knew it was finished.
Now he is in pieces,
he has not spoken
since Thursday night.

He is dazed,
confused,
grief-stricken.

Was it really only a week ago
that we walked beside the donkey
waving to cheering crowds
proud to be with the Messiah
proud to be seen by his side?
It was another lifetime
It was a different dream.

We are lost without Jesus,
our focus,
our solid centre
our catalyst,
our link with God.

Peter and Andrew want to make plans
to look to the future
but how can we?
How can we return to fishing,
tax collecting, farming?

We have glimpsed the brightness of hope
of the Kingdom
How can we return
to the mundane routine
of the everyday?

We are torn apart
by grief and shock
frustrated by this enforced rest.
The jars of oil are waiting by the door
waiting for us
for the end of the Sabbath
so that we can do this one last thing

pay our last respects
before we move on
or back
or away.

For now,
all we can do is wait,
and wonder
and worry
that every knock at the door
is more bad news,
that every footfall in the street below
are those of soldiers coming to arrest us.
We hide in dark corners
and speak in whispers
until passion makes our voices rise
to be anxiously hushed
by frightened friends.

We are too terrified to pray.
We cannot find the words.
We dare not believe we will be heard.
Why should we?
Jesus' last words,
screamed in anguish
stop our belief,
and are a barrier to our trust
that God will hear us
when He did not listen to His Messiah.

The jars by the door speak of tomorrow.
But I can't think of tomorrow.
It will bring new challenges, shocks and griefs,
and I cannot take any more.
I want to stay with today
where there can be no more surprises,

no more shocks
or challenges to be overcome,
only known shock
and overwhelming, numbing grief.

I want to stay here,
cocooned in grief,
lost in memories,
longing to wake from this nightmare.

I want to go back
to when I was listening to Jesus
teaching by the lake,
walking with him along the road
discussing his parables.
I want to be beside the colt,
amidst the cheering crowds.

I don't want to be here,
waiting
with nothing to do
but remember
and grieve.

God our Maker, you are here,
waiting with us when things are uncertain
and we do not know where to turn.

Jesus our Saviour, you are here beside us,
understanding why we find waiting so hard
and are impatient for answers.

Spirit of Compassion, you are here within us,
helping us to support one another without recriminations.

We are God's People, trusting in God, waiting in faith.

EASTER

unending beginnings

31   The Courage To Overcome Fear

When the Sabbath was over, Mary Magdalene, and Mary the mother of James, and Salome bought spices, so that they might go and anoint him. And very early on the first day of the week, when the sun had risen, they went to the tomb. They had been saying to one another, "Who will roll away the stone for us from the entrance to the tomb?" When they looked up, they saw that the stone, which was very large, had already been rolled back. As they entered the tomb, they saw a young man, dressed in a white robe, sitting on the right side; and they were alarmed. But he said to them,

"Do not be alarmed; you are looking for Jesus of Nazareth, who was crucified. He has been raised; he is not here. Look, there is the place they laid him. But go, tell his disciples and Peter that he is going ahead of you to Galilee; there you will see him, just as he told you."

So they went out and fled from the tomb, for they were afraid.

Mark 16:1-8

The abrupt end of Mark's Gospel has prompted much debate, not least because the original Greek ends with a preposition "They went out and fled from the tomb, for they were afraid of…" There has been speculation about why they were afraid, or of what, and why Mark chose to end his Gospel in this way. From a human perspective it is easy to understand why they would have been afraid. They had just encountered a heavenly messenger telling them that Jesus had been raised from the dead. They would be struggling to understand, to take in the import of the words as well as the implications for themselves and the disciples. During the long Saturday of waiting they would have been coming to terms with their loss, adjusting their thinking and their plans to accommodate Jesus' death. Suddenly they have been given news that throws all that into confusion, and are afraid of the future, afraid of the unknown. What would the risen Jesus want of them? And how would they find the words to tell the other disciples, to convince them that they were not hysterical or dreaming?

Fear can be paralysing, stopping us from moving forward or taking risks and it takes great courage to overcome that fear and trust that change can be for the better and that resurrection is possible. Fear can paralyse and prevent us from taking the next step into an unknown future, precisely because it is unknown. Although Mark does not recount how the women told the disciples, they must have done, or the Church would not exist. Somehow Jesus' resurrection gave them the courage to overcome their fear and embrace the change of plan that came with it. Where fear of the unknown holds us back, the voices of the women at the tomb call us forward to embrace new possibilities.

For They Were Afraid
The Women: We were afraid.
               We couldn't find the words
               to explain what we had seen
               what we'd heard
               what we'd felt.

               Who would believe us?
               Who would listen?
               We're just a bunch of hysterical women
               unable to cope with reality.

               We were afraid
               of being patronised
               or belittled
               or dismissed as liars.

               It is easier for everyone
               if we keep to our roles,
               if we conform to society's norms
               for grieving women
               and distraught friends.

166

People will know how to react
what to say
what to do.
It is safe,
for them
and for us.

How can we find the words
to express this shock
this change
this impossible miracle?

We saw him die,
we heard his last cry
but now he's alive!

How can we explain,
how can we describe it?
No one will listen.
No one will believe
a group of grieving women.

But we must find the words.
It is burning inside us
bursting to get out.

We *must* be heard.
We *must* be believed.
It has happened.
New Life is here!
Stereotypes can be broken
Resurrection is possible.
Even for us!

God our Maker, you are here,
surprising us with new life
and rolling away the stones that block our paths.

Risen Christ, you are here beside us,
demonstrating that there are no stereotypes that cannot be broken
and no need to be held back by convention.

Life-Giving Spirit, you are here within us,
encouraging us to break free of our fears
and shout out the good news of new life in Christ.

We are God's People, individually cherished for our uniqueness and
held together by the love of God.

32   Called By My Name

But Mary stood weeping outside the tomb. As she wept, she bent over to look into the tomb; and she saw two angels in white, sitting where the body of Jesus had been lying, one at the head and the other at the feet. They said to her, "Woman, why are you weeping?" She said to them, "They have taken away my Lord, and I do not know where they have laid him." When she had said this, she turned around and saw Jesus standing there, but she did not know that it was Jesus. Jesus said to her, "Woman, why are you weeping? Whom are you looking for?" Supposing him to be the gardener, she said to him, "Sir, if you have carried him away, tell me where you have laid him, and I will take him away."

Jesus said to her, "Mary!" She turned and said to him in Hebrew, "Rabbouni!" (which means Teacher).

John 20:11-16

John's Gospel describes Easter morning from the perspective of Mary Magdalene. She came to the tomb first and discovered that the stone had been rolled away, so she went to fetch Peter and John. They went into the tomb and discovered the discarded linen cloths in which Jesus' body had been wrapped, but according to John did not fully understand what had happened. When they returned home, Mary remained behind, weeping. She had come to pay her respects and to lay out his body with the oils she had carefully prepared. She was distressed because she could not perform this last act of love and in her pain did not want to leave the tomb where she had last seen him. When she encountered the risen Jesus, it was only when he called her by her name that she recognised him.

The use of our given name rather than a nickname or a label derived from our condition or occupation is an act of respect and love. It is very easy to fall into bad habits of addressing people or dealing with them according to labels or nicknames which reflect only part of their character. For people with health issues, whether mental or physical, being treated as a person rather than a condition is recognition that we are not defined by it. It is liberating because it demonstrates that we are more than a label, more than our health issues, we are loved and valued as human beings, not as a scientific case study. Jesus called Mary by her name so that she could see that resurrection, change and healing was possible, especially when we are valued enough to be called by our name.

He Called Me By My Name
Mary: He called me by my name
gently
lovingly
encouragingly.

He did not give me a label
and call me
"hysterical"
"unbalanced"
or "delusional"
dismissing me
as a hopeless case.

He called me by my name
recognised me
welcomed me
wanted to speak to me!

He did not ignore me
or look beyond me
for someone more reliable
someone of greater worth
someone others would believe.

He called *me* by *my* name
not the names that others use
that make me weep with shame

or scream with despair
because they do not see me,
only a problem
to be handled with care.

He used *my* name
the one that tells me
that I am treasured
that I have dignity
that I am valued
and wanted.

He called me by my name
and I recognised him,
in the warmth of his voice
the healing of his welcome
and the hope in my heart.

He called me by my name
and now I praise His.

God our Maker, you are here,
calling us by our name,
loving us for who we are.

Risen Christ, you are here beside us,
welcoming us with love.

Life-Giving Spirit, you are here within us,
bringing us hope and strength.

We are God's People, called by name, witnesses of new life.

33 The Courage to Talk

> Now on that same day two of them were going to a village called Emmaus, about seven miles from Jerusalem, and talking with each other about all these things that had happened. While they were talking and discussing, Jesus himself came near and went with them, but their eyes were kept from recognizing him.
>
> *Luke 24: 13-14*

The two disciples who were returning to Emmaus are not identified as members of the Twelve, but the implication is that they had been closely involved with the events of Holy Week. The reason for their journey is not given, but it is generally assumed that they came from Emmaus and were going home. As they walked, they discussed what had happened, trying to make sense of it between themselves.

This scene is one that is familiar to us because whenever we witness momentous events we want to talk about them to help us process our emotions and to understand what we have seen. We often find it easiest to talk to those who have shared the experience so that we can compare notes and exchange theories without having to explain ourselves. The problem with this is that our vision can be so clouded by what has happened and the endless repetition of events can overwhelm us with grief and trauma that we lose our sense of perspective and are unable to move forward.

It is harder to talk to someone we don't know, such as a counsellor or therapist, as we need to explain things from the beginning. It takes time to trust them because there is no bond of shared experience and we may be afraid of being told that we are worrying about nothing. But a stranger can stand outside the experience and look beyond the hurt to point out God's plan of enduring love.

We Understood

Cleopas -   We felt let down
it was foolish to have believed
all that talk of new life.
It was folly to have trusted
the teaching about the New Kingdom.
We were dazzled by the healings,
filled with hope by his new ideas
we really thought he was the Messiah.

But he was a charlatan
no better than the rest,
claiming powers that were not real
proclaiming events that will not happen.

We had left Jerusalem
turned our backs on faith
because we could not take any more.
Some were talking about resurrection,
but how could he come back to life?
We wanted no more lies
no more false hope,
so we walked away,
exhausted and disappointed,
returning home
to failure and ridicule.

We'd hoped to see a new beginning
but all we'd seen was the end
of all our hopes and dreams.
It was so hard to face the truth.
We went over it again and again
trying to understand,
trying to find a way to be certain
whether we were right
or wrong.

174

We talked a bit, argued a lot
because we couldn't understand
what had gone wrong.

We discussed the impossible
rumours
that this was a new beginning.
I wanted to believe it
but was told off
for clutching at straws.

"They were wrong," I fumed
"and stupid to believe in fairy tales.
 We were right to leave,
 right to give up
 on impossible promises."

I was frustrated,
and raging with disappointment
because I felt I had been foolish,
and I hate to be publicly humiliated.

I don't know
when the stranger joined us,
we were so deep in discussion
arguing again
about what had happened
and why
that we didn't see him,
but suddenly he was there
listening to our confusion
absorbing our anger
and despair.

He joined in our conversation
asked questions about what had happened.
It was incredible

how could he not know
the only topic of conversation in the country.

So we explained
and he listened
and he probed
and he suggested
and he knew his Scripture.

This patient stranger,
who listened
and talked us out of our arguments
and away from the hopeless circle
of pointless repetition,
pointed us towards God,
and new life.
He corrected our hindsight
altered our blinkered vision
and the mists of confusion
began to clear.
Hope was reignited
and faith flickered into life.

Suddenly,
dented pride did not matter
being wrong was irrelevant.
We were no longer tired,
no longer angry,
no longer hopeless.

What mattered was keeping faith
and keeping going.
What mattered was having the courage
to admit that we were wrong
and going back to start again.
Hope and faith do not give up
and neither should we.

God our Maker, you are here,
creating time for discussion
and learning from one another.

Risen Christ, you are here beside us,
walking with us, even when we do not recognise you
gently leading us where we need to go.

Life-Giving Spirit, you are here within us,
helping us to learn from the past without guilt or recrimination
and walk forward into the future with faith.

We are God's People, always walking with God, and always listening
for God's word.

34   Encouraged By The Familiar

As they came near the village to which they were going, he walked ahead as if he were going on. But they urged him strongly, saying, "Stay with us, because it is almost evening and the day is now nearly over." So he went in to stay with them. When he was at the table with them, he took bread, blessed and broke it, and gave it to them. Then their eyes were opened, and they recognized him; and he vanished from their sight.

That same hour they got up and returned to Jerusalem; and they found the eleven and their companions gathered together. Then they told what had happened on the road, and how he had been made known to them in the breaking of the bread.

Luke 24: 28-31, 33, 35

It can be frustrating when we get the feeling that we know someone but are unable to recall their name or from where we know them. Nothing will bring this information to our mind until they do or say something that unlocks the puzzle. This was what happened to the two disciples who had walked back to Emmaus with Jesus. Despite the long conversation that could have revealed his identity, despite having been told that Jesus had risen from the dead, they didn't recognise Jesus until he broke the bread at supper. This action was so familiar to them that "their eyes were opened" and they realised who he was. With that revelation came the realisation that he had kept his promise of new life and that gave them the strength to get up and return to Jerusalem.

Familiar phrases, objects and actions can bring us great comfort as an anchor when we are surrounded by constant change and uncertainty that challenges or frightens us. This need for the familiar object is most frequently seen when young children cling to a favourite toy or blanket as a reassurance that they have not been abandoned and a reminder that they are loved. Many people carry forward the need for the familiar into adulthood by having a talisman in a pocket or investing significance in an item of clothing by having "lucky socks". The objects are less obvious than a teddy bear or a comfort blanket, but they still remind us of happy memories and reassure us of being loved and help us to feel secure when faced with the unfamiliar.

Many people with mental health issues seem to need constant reassurance of the familiar and ask for constant repetition of words of support, value and understanding which can be wearing on the care-giver. Once we understand that their condition and/or the therapeutic treatment they receive can take them into difficult, dangerous and painful places, we can begin to understand the need for the familiar. They need reminders of promises made and kept so that they have the strength to face the unfamiliar and challenging, just as the Emmaus disciples needed the reassurance of Jesus breaking the bread to have the strength to leave the familiarity of home and take up the unknown challenges of discipleship.

Our Eyes Were Opened
Hannah:
> He seemed familiar as he walked with us.
> We felt comfortable as he talked with us.
> So we asked him to share a meal
> to thank him for his help,
> and in an old familiar action
> we recognised him,
> the real him,
> whose promises
> we had always trusted.

> It was reassuringly familiar
> reminding us of earlier times
> of promises made and kept,
> of friendships cemented
> in shared experiences
> in the breaking of bread
> for the hungry,

for the thousands of followers on a hillside,
and the last time, in Jerusalem,
just for us.

It was the reassurance
of continued love
and unending support
in a simple, familiar, routine gesture
that said "You matter"
"You are loved."

It was the reassurance we needed
to face the unknown
to leave behind our doubts
and return to the others
and the new life ahead.

God our Maker, you are here,
creating times of reflection and recognition
that let us see you at work in our lives .

Risen Christ, you are here beside us,
revealing yourself in everyday gestures and places,
reassuring us that we are not alone.

Life-Giving Spirit, you are here within us,
giving us the strength to go back and try again
even when we have felt that it was useless.

We are God's People, alight with hope
and overflowing with faith in the God who never leaves us.

35   Love That Sees No Barriers

> When it was evening on that day, the first day of the week, and the doors of the house where the disciples had met were locked for fear of the Jews, Jesus came and stood among them and said, "Peace be with you." After he said this, he showed them his hands and his side. Then the disciples rejoiced when they saw the Lord.
>
> *John 20:19-20, 24-27*

The most telling comment in this passage is "the doors were locked for fear of the Jews". Many mental health problems are driven by fear – fear of failure, fear of imperfection, fear of letting down others, fear of not being good enough, fear of past events recurring. And the response of many who do not understand mental health issues is fear. It is not easy to understand what is going on in someone else's head, and the response to unusual behaviour is fear of the effect it will have on others.

When the fear becomes overwhelming, like the disciples, we lock ourselves away in secure places where that which we fear cannot reach us. It is like coming home at the end of a busy or stressful day, closing the curtains, locking the door and shutting out the world in a place where we feel safe and unthreatened. Sometimes, like the disciples, we don't want to have to fight prejudice or justify ourselves to anyone else, we just want to be with those who have walked the same road, who understand.

Yet, just as Jesus broke through the locked doors to bring the disciples peace, so he breaks through our barriers to give us peace and strength, and the resilience to keep taking risks, to face our fears, to continue to walk alongside those who struggle. When we feel unreachable and unlovable, God breaks in and shows us his wounds, and says, "I came through, and with my help, you will too."

Behind Locked Doors

    Barricaded by nightmares
of past events
Cowering behind terror
of imperfection
Hiding from demons
of lost control
Unable to break free
to unlock the door
to allow light
into the darkness of fear.

Shrinking into a corner,
seeking security
in obscurity.
Imprisoned by fear
of the future
of failure
of the past
Unable to reach out
and take steps of trust
to have faith
to believe.

Words of comfort
in the midst of a storm
pushed aside
by darkening clouds
of suspicion and disbelief.
Healing moments
of paralysis released
and blindness unshuttered
forgotten, unheeded,
swamped by self-doubt
drowned out by critical voices.

Yet, even through the barriers
that shut out the pain of the world
that cushion sores
and shield them from more damage,
breaking through the locks
that protect the frightened soul
shattering false illusions
and dispelling the dark clouds
is the risen Christ,
whom the disciples recognised
as Jesus.

The same Jesus
who encouraged Peter
to do the impossible;
who silenced a storm
of critical voices
with understanding and
forgiveness;
who reached out to the outcast
and drew them in;
who liberated prisoners
from tormenting demons;
who showed that
perfect love
loves imperfection;
that defeat is not a failure
but a chance to try again;
and that God rejoices in the ordinary
the average,
and the commonplace.

His words of greeting
are not criticism but comfort.
"Peace be with you."

Peace to still the storm,
Peace to quieten demons,
Peace to have courage,
Peace to take risks,
Peace,
wherever it is needed.

God our Maker, you are here,
breaking down the barriers we have created to keep ourselves safe.

Risen Christ, you are here beside us,
showing that not even death can keep out your love or your new life.

Life-Giving Spirit, you are here within us,
helping us to hear the healing words of peace.

We are God's People, strengthened and encouraged by Christ's
presence among us.

36   The Courage To Admit Doubt

But Thomas (who was called the Twin), one of the twelve, was not with them when Jesus came. So the other disciples told him, "We have seen the Lord." But he said to them, "Unless I see the mark of the nails in his hands, and put my finger in the mark of the nails and my hand in his side, I will not believe."

A week later his disciples were again in the house, and Thomas was with them. Although the doors were shut, Jesus came and stood among them and said, "Peace be with you." Then he said to Thomas, "Put your finger here and see my hands. Reach out your hand and put it in my side. Do not doubt but believe." Thomas answered him, "My Lord and my God!"

John 20: 24-28

History has been hard on Thomas. He has been given the epithet "Doubting" for having the honesty to admit that he was being asked to believe the impossible. Peer pressure is a hidden but very persuasive force to conform. It must have taken a great deal of courage to go against the very obvious faith of the others in the room and admit that he didn't understand enough to believe them. The other disciples may have teased Thomas, or ignored him, or spent hours pointing out the error of his ways.

Those who are struggling with confusion and grief, as Thomas was, are often also assailed by doubts about issues that have not previously been questioned. When we voice doubts about our faith, other members of our faith community can feel threatened or too challenged to face them, and either deny the question or tell us that we are wrong to ask it. All faiths need doubt to stimulate exploration and discussion, to encourage honesty and understanding, but it is often ignored or condemned as divisive. So the courage to admit that we are not convinced, to ask for further debate or evidence can leave us out on a limb or ostracised for daring to think differently, meaning that admitting doubt in the face of overwhelming faith can be isolating, especially in a small community.

This meditation offers another perspective on Thomas' doubts by trying to understand the depth of pain that led him to say "unless I put my hand in his side". He had witnessed Jesus' crucifixion and seen not only how he died, but also that he had died. It is perfectly understandable that Thomas would have struggled to credit that someone who had sustained those appalling injuries could be alive. Our doubts when faced with indescribable pain and challenge should be likewise acceptable. After all, Jesus' response to Thomas' honesty is neither censure nor rejection, but loving reassurance.

I Couldn't Believe

Thomas: I couldn't believe the others,
      Dare not believe them,
      How could I?

      I stood and watched him die.
      How can he now be alive?
      I saw the nails driven through his hands
      I heard his cry of anguish
      and abandonment.
      I watched them plunge the spear
      deep into his side.

      When others turned away
      unable to bear it any longer
      I stayed, I saw,
      He suffered
      He died,
      How can he be alive?

      So I couldn't believe the others
      I couldn't believe they had forgotten
      the agony of his last breath
      the blood flowing from his side.
      He couldn't have survived that
      couldn't have come back,

however much they wanted it,
however much they believed it.

I had seen his suffering.
I had heard his despair.
No longer the man of strength,
but a frightened, beaten man.

Even if he came back
it could not be
as it was before
with him as our rock,
our shepherd, our guide.
How could it be
when we had seen him vulnerable?
I couldn't believe it,
however much they insisted.

And then he was there
showing me his wounds
inviting me to touch them
to believe again.

And then I believed,
because then I knew
then I understood
what it was all about.

He was not coming back
as if nothing had happened
to continue
as if agony does not matter.

He came back *because* of the agony
He came back *with* the scars
of hate,
of prejudice,
of fear.

He came back
to show that they could not win
that even these scars
cannot stop God from loving
and must not stop us from living.

He came back,
despite my disbelief.
I didn't need to touch him
to know he was really there.
I saw his compassion
I saw his strength
I saw his grace.
I saw my Lord and my God.

> *God our Maker, you are here,*
> *creating opportunities for deepening our understanding of you.*
>
> *Risen Christ, you are here beside us,*
> *leading us gently to the truths of new life we need to hear.*
>
> *Life-Giving Spirit, you are here within us,*
> *opening our eyes and minds to the reality of a well-loved life.*
>
> *We are God's People, valued and cherished by God, in our doubt as well as our faith.*

37   Retreating To A Safe Place

Gathered there together were Simon Peter, Thomas called the Twin, Nathanael of Cana in Galilee, the sons of Zebedee, and two others of his disciples. Simon Peter said to them, "I am going fishing." They said to him, "We will go with you." They went out and got into the boat, but that night they caught nothing.

Just after daybreak, Jesus stood on the beach; but the disciples did not know that it was Jesus. Jesus said to them, "Children, you have no fish, have you?" They answered him, "No."

He said to them, "Cast the net to the right side of the boat, and you will find some." So they cast it, and now they were not able to haul it in because there were so many fish.   That disciple whom Jesus loved said to Peter, "It is the Lord!" When Simon Peter heard that it was the Lord, he put on some clothes, for he was naked, and jumped into the sea.

John 21:2-7

It seems as though the disciples were at a loose end. When Jesus died, they had lost their leader who had made all the decisions about what to do and where to go. As they waited for what was to happen next, they returned to somewhere familiar and to something they understood. We all know the comfort we find in known places and routines where we can remind ourselves of our roots or skills we have previously honed. It brings us comfort when we have been traumatised and is a way of escaping from the challenge and fear of the unknown.

There can be a parallel with those who are struggling when they return to the cause of their distress, finding safety in known grief and behaviours. It is easier and less challenging to stay with the known, however painful, than to let go and move on. When comfort is needed, tried and tested behaviours, such as tears of abandonment can produce the expected response of reassurance and love that answer the needs. When the response is not what is expected, it produces anxiety and stress, but can also trigger release from a downward spiral. The disciples in the boat would have been dispirited that they had caught nothing, and when the figure from the shore acknowledged their failure, they would have expected either commiseration or laughter. However, the response was a suggestion that they try a different way, a more fruitful way. That was what revealed to the beloved disciple that it was Jesus on the shore, showing the way to new life.

Going Fishing

John: Peter said he was going fishing
        There was nothing else to do.
        Our future had so radically changed,
        the way forward seemed blocked
        by uncertainty
        and lack of direction,
        it seemed easier to go back
        than to move forward,
        so we went with him.

        We assumed it would be easy
        that we'd still remember the tricks
        but it wasn't as familiar as we'd thought.
        Even though we sailed all night
        searching for shoals
        peering into the darkness
        looking for signs of life,
        we saw nothing.

        We fell silent
        too exhausted for further bickering
        about whose fault it was,
        but not willing to give up
        not prepared to admit failure.

        We didn't even want to distract ourselves
        by talking about the past weeks.
        We put all our effort

into staying afloat
and all our strength
into steering a sensible course.

At dawn we saw a figure on the shore.
We tried to ignore him.
We didn't want interference
or a witness to our incompetence.
But he persisted
so we had to respond
and trust his different perspective.

And then I realised
what I should have already known.
I turned to Peter and told him
and he leapt overboard
and splashed ashore.

We should have known
that God who comes through locked doors
will also find us from the darkness of a lake shore
when we have retreated to our safe space.

He found us,
and encouraged us
to see what was there
and what we could achieve.
He called us back to shore
fed us and strengthened us
to face life again.

God our Maker, you are here,
creating safe places when we need rest
and new opportunities when we need to be challenged.

Risen Christ, you are here beside us,
showing us that there is nowhere that is beyond God's reach.

Life-Giving Spirit, you are here within us,
encouraging us to move into new places
and leave behind safe harbours
so that we learn more about God's love.

We are God's People, created for new experiences, and always within
God's sight and hold.

38   Love Is Enough

Jesus said to them, "Come and have breakfast." Now none of the disciples dared to ask him, "Who are you?" because they knew it was the Lord. Jesus came and took the bread and gave it to them, and did the same with the fish.

When they had finished breakfast, Jesus said to Simon Peter, "Simon son of John, do you love me more than these?" He said to him, "Yes, Lord; you know that I love you." Jesus said to him, "Feed my lambs." A second time he said to him, "Simon son of John, do you love me?" He said to him, "Yes, Lord; you know that I love you." Jesus said to him, "Tend my sheep." He said to him the third time, "Simon son of John, do you love me?" Peter felt hurt because he said to him the third time, "Do you love me?" And he said to him, "Lord, you know everything; you know that I love you." Jesus said to him, "Feed my sheep. [...] After this he said to him, "Follow me."

John 21: 12-13,15-17, 19

The most simple interpretation of this encounter between Peter and the risen Christ is that the threefold repetition of "Do you love me?" was a counterbalance to Peter's threefold denial of Jesus in the courtyard. Jesus then reinstated Peter as one of his loyal followers. It is a wonderful illustration of Jesus' forgiveness and the possibility of redemption. And it is a practical demonstration of how redemption can work. Jesus not only forgave Peter, he also told him how best to demonstrate that love. Instead of just letting Peter continue in his old way of loving, Jesus instructed him to "Feed my sheep."

It is easy when dealing with the difficult and awkward moment of forgiveness to just accept an apology without discussing some of the deeper issues that may have led to the problem in the first place. The adage "least said, soonest mended" is not always the best advice as it can lead to resentments being buried. These then fester and erupt in a much more serious way at a later date. True redemption is about demonstrating or discussing how to proceed in the future to avoid the same pain being caused again.

Care-givers for people with mental health issues will be aware that they need to be clear about their boundaries. Whilst reassuring those for whom they care that they are still loved, they need to give guidance on how to keep the relationship healthy and as balanced as possible. They give advice on how best to love others that is not about engulfing people with gifts or demanding constant, instant communication. It is more loving to have an honest conversation that respects the sufferer's capacity to make choices, than to dismiss the overwhelming needs as irredeemable and irrevocable. Redemption comes through trusting the loving relationship and giving the sufferer room to grow and learn.

Do You Love Me?

Peter: He talked so often
        about forgiveness.
        Told me to forgive
        "Seventy times seven"
        "I can't count that high"
        I told him.
        "So don't try," he smiled
        "Just keep on forgiving."

I didn't really understand
didn't really know true forgiveness
until I faced him
and my failure.

At first there was nothing but joy.
I rushed up to him
overpowered by the need to see him.

But after the initial excitement
I was haunted by my denials
and my rejection of his friendship
just to save my own skin.

When he called me over
I braced myself for anger
for disappointment and recrimination
but received only gentleness,
and a challenge - "Do you love me?"

What a question
when I've just rushed up to him,
waded through freezing water,
heart overflowing that he has come back.
"Do you love me?"
Three times he asked me,
three times that showed me
that love is enough.
Then I was challenged
to reaffirm my commitment
to declare my love for him,
and shown how to love him better.

Now I understand
what he has always been saying –
that love is enough.
Love is strong enough to face the problems,
to heal hurts and bring hope
when we are strong enough to be honest.
Love is strong enough,
to turn away from hurt,
to plan a way forward,
to risk everything,
for someone else,
for God love is enough.

God our Maker, you are here,
creating times of joy and reconciliation.

Risen Christ, you are here beside us,
showing us that healing is possible
and that relationships can be rebuilt.

Life-Giving Spirit, you are here within us,
enabling us to reach out in forgiveness and hope
to build bridges of trust and understanding
where we have previously destroyed them.

We are God's People, forgiven and renewed
by the healing power of love.

39   The Courage To Trust

Now the eleven disciples went to Galilee, to the mountain to which Jesus had directed them. And Jesus came and said to them, "All authority in heaven and on earth has been given to me. Go therefore and make disciples of all nations, baptizing them in the name of the Father and of the Son and of the Holy Spirit, and teaching them to obey everything that I have commanded you. And remember, I am with you always, to the end of the age."

Matthew 28: 16, 18-20

Matthew's account of Jesus' final words to his disciples is a great message of hope. This is not just because of his assurance that he will be with them always, but also because he returned to a group of friends who had deserted him, been afraid of being associated with him, denied him, and doubted the truth of his message. Despite all this, he is still willing to entrust them with the future of the Kingdom. Throughout his earthly ministry, however many times the disciples got it wrong, misunderstood him or misrepresented him, Jesus always understood and forgave them. His words of farewell are not just a seemingly impossible demand "Make disciples of all nations" but also an act of incredible grace and trust as he hands over his ministry to them.

Jesus knew he was asking a lot of the disciples when he asked them to trust him after all they had experienced in the past weeks. He knew they had been to the limits of emotions and the depths of despair, and then challenged to accept a new way of understanding the power of God. He also knew that despite his reassurances of forgiveness since his resurrection, still at the back of their minds may have hovered the memory of how they had let him down. Despite their doubts and their exhaustion, he demonstrated that he believed them trustworthy, and promised that he would never abandon them.

There is a basic human need to trust and be trusted which is the foundation of all our relationships. And rebuilding trust is one of the hardest challenges we face when relationships have broken down or been through an incredibly testing time, such as a mental health episode. When promises have been broken, our emotions have been wrung dry, or we are in the depths of despair, we are wary of being hurt again, of trusting promises or believing in recovery or hoping for joy. Being trusted, as the disciples were on the Mount of Ascension, is an incredibly healing experience, because it restores self-worth and confidence. The existence of the Church, built on the work of the eleven men to whom Jesus entrusted his Kingdom, witnesses to that. And the promise they were given, "Remember, I am with you always, to the end of the age" is also a promise to us, that when we reach out in trust, and take risks, we are not on our own.

Go Into All The World
Philip: "Trust me," he said
         as if nothing had happened
         as if it was a parable
         that taught us about the Kingdom,
         or an impossible miracle
         or a journey to a new town.

         "Trust me,"
         as if the last few weeks
         had not been the most distressing,
         most confusing,
         most turbulent of our lives.
         One minute living in fear,
         the next engulfed by grief,
         then inexplicable joy,
         and misunderstanding and trepidation,
         and hope.

         "Trust me,"
         as if he hadn't been the cause
         of the turmoil
         the confusion

the hurt
the betrayal,
the indomitable hope.

I looked at the others.
Would we trust this promise?
They looked back at me
and in the eyes of the deserters
the deniers and the doubters
the frightened and the sceptical
there was disbelief,
trepidation,
joy and hope.

"Trust me,
  for I am entrusting you
  with my Kingdom."

He trusts us?
Us, his fickle friends?
Those who have let him down,
who ran away when he needed us,
who pretended we had never known him,
who could not even pray with him
in his loneliest hour,
HE trusts US
with his most precious work
his Kingdom?

And then he'd done it again,
turned our world upside down.
Suddenly it was not about our trust in him,
but his in us.
It was another impossible miracle
of new life and hope,
another parable of the Kingdom
that taught of redemption,

another journey in his footsteps
to another town,
another place,
another country.
As understanding dawned
and hope and joy burned brighter
knowing that we were forgiven,
knowing that we were trusted,
how could we not return trust
with trust?

"Trust me,
 You won't be abandoned.
 You will have strength,
 you will have the words
 you will not be on your own."

"I trust you,
 I will always trust you
 no matter how many times you fail
 or run away.
 Trust me,
 for I will be with you always
 even to the end of time."

God our Maker, you are here,
creating bridges of trust between us.

Living Christ, you are here beside us,
demonstrating that trust can be renewed
and hope reborn.

Life-Giving Spirit, you are here within us,
helping us to fulfil the commission of trust we have been given by
Christ.

We are God's People, sent by Christ
and enabled by the Spirit to build Christ's Kingdom of Love .

40   The Courage To Begin Again

Meanwhile Saul, still breathing threats and murder against the disciples of the Lord, went to the high priest and asked him for letters to the synagogues at Damascus, so that if he found any who belonged to the Way, men or women, he might bring them bound to Jerusalem. Now as he was going along and approaching Damascus, suddenly a light from heaven flashed around him. He fell to the ground and heard a voice saying to him, "Saul, Saul, why do you persecute me?" He asked, "Who are you, Lord?"

The reply came, "I am Jesus, whom you are persecuting. But get up and enter the city, and you will be told what you are to do."

The men who were travelling with him stood speechless because they heard the voice but saw no one. Saul got up from the ground, and though his eyes were open, he could see nothing; so they led him by the hand and brought him into Damascus. For three days he was without sight, and neither ate nor drank.

Ananias went and entered the house. He laid his hands on Saul and said, "Brother Saul, the Lord Jesus, who appeared to you on your way here, has sent me so that you may regain your sight and be filled with the Holy Spirit." And immediately something like scales fell from his eyes, and his sight was restored. Then he got up and was baptized, and after taking some food, he regained his strength. For several days he was with the disciples in Damascus, and immediately he began to proclaim Jesus in the synagogues, saying, "He is the Son of God."

Acts 9:1-9, 17-20

The story of Saul's conversion and his later ministry as Paul the apostle is another instance of the incredible grace of God. Saul, a man who is actively pursuing and persecuting Christians, encounters the risen Christ and is challenged to make a complete about turn with his life and faith, and become a leader in the organisation he used to despise. God's grace is not only shown in Christ's encounter with Saul on the road to

Damascus and his later healing by Ananias, but also in the disciples in the town who welcomed Saul without suspicion. Saul/Paul also demonstrates immense grace when he is able to go to the leaders of the Church whom he has persecuted and admit that he was wrong and ask to be admitted into their number. It is never easy to admit that we have been wrong, especially when we have been very public with our views, so Paul needed immense courage to face Peter and the other apostles. If his epistles reflect his attitude accurately, then he would say that he was only able to do that by the grace of God acting on him and in him.

For those who have had a mental health episode that has led them to do or say things without being fully aware of what they were doing, the later remembrance or discussion and of these actions can make them feel ashamed or embarrassed. This makes going back to places where they have been critical or dismissed friendships as worthless is hard. It can be equally hard to return to therapy or go back onto medication when it has seemed they have been dismissed as unnecessary because the sufferer can cope without them. And it's not easy being wrong when we care for people who are struggling, when they lash out at us or when we offer advice that we later discover has been unhelpful. What is needed in every case is the grace to admit we were wrong, and the grace to accept the apology without recriminations and look to the future rather than the past.

It's Not Easy, Being Wrong.

Paul: It's not easy, being wrong.
        Admitting I'm at fault,
        begging someone's pardon,
        asking forgiveness,
        is not something
        that I do.

        I was brought up to privilege,
        status,
        and the assurance of being right
        and unchallenged.

That means
never having to apologise,
admit fault,
or beg forgiveness.

And yet,
I have had to learn
how to be humble
how to be forgiven.

What amazes me
is that I am forgiven,
not only forgiven
but accepted
welcomed
and enfolded into the community.

I burn with shame
when I remember
the cutting remarks.

I shrivel inside
when I recall the hate
that drove me to hurt
and the fear
that fuelled my anger
and spite.

These people,
whom I have hurt
and tried to destroy
over whose feelings I rode
with unthinking arrogance
and whose beliefs I trampled
beneath contemptuous feet,
have forgiven me

for the sake of the one
who stopped me in my tracks
and made me see
that a new life,
a better way,
was not only possible
but also necessary.

Despite all I have done
they have believed me
believed in me
and in my change of heart.

They do not remind me
of who I was
and how I was
but instead
they encourage me
pray for me
welcome me
for who I am now
and who I can become
through the grace of God.

God our Maker, you are here,
creating opportunities to begin again where we have previously failed.

Living Christ, you are here beside us,
showing that resurrection and new life is possible,
even in the most painful situations.

Life-Giving Spirit, you are here within us,
prompting us to reach out and help
those trying to make amends and begin again.

We are God's People, living in the light of God's resurrection hope.

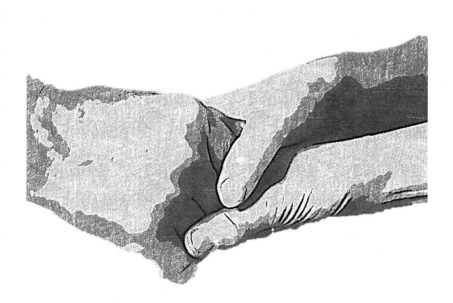

Epilogue

Through planning and writing these meditations, I have discovered what great strength can be gained from realising that Jesus did run through the entire spectrum of emotions in his lifetime. Although this work has focussed on Holy Week and the very extreme emotions experienced by Jesus and his followers, the Gospel narratives of Jesus' ministry portray a very human man who understood every part of human life and emotion. The importance of this for us is that he understands how we feel, and that gives us the strength to respond as his disciples, however broken, rather than as fallible and hurting human beings.

The place where Jesus' suffering is most evident is on the cross, but the place to which I find myself returning most is the table where he instituted the New Covenant of grace. And he did it knowing that those at the table would betray him, desert him and deny him at a time when he most needed them, yet he did not exclude them. For me that shows the immensity of God's grace, that forgives and understands despite the excruciating agony of what is to come. I find at the table a strength to take on the Christ-like self and return grace for grudge, love for selfishness and hope for despair. It is not an easy strength, it does not come without personal cost, as Jesus demonstrates so clearly in his cry of dereliction from the cross. What can help us to get through the pain is the knowledge that we are not alone, and that God will give us grace to forgive, just as he forgave those who came to the Last Supper, and be given another chance, just as they were.

It was important that the last ten meditations were included to show that the disciples did experience renewal of hope and faith, that Jesus did, and does reassure us that we are forgiven for falling down, for failing, for being human. These meditations are not designed to resolve the emotions we feel, they are to reassure us that God, through Jesus Christ, is with us in all things. Whether we turn to Jesus on the cross, his silence in front of Pilate, or the table of the New Covenant, we find hope that this is not the end, that in the strength of Christ resurrection is possible.

Sharing communion with those who have hurt us, or who turn away from us because of the problems we cause, is not easy. This final meditation was written in 2012 as a response to the hymn "For everyone born, a place at the table", which suggests that kneeling at the table we would find both "abuser and abused with need to forgive". It tries to express the difficulty of kneeling at the communion table beside those who have hurt us, or to administer the sacrament to those who belittle and betray us. Through writing it, I came to realise that however much we want to assuage our own hurt and guilt by excluding others, that is not the way of God. The only way to save ourselves from the hurt we feel is to acknowledge it before God, and accept that he understands it, and offers us the chance of resurrection.

A Place At The Table
There is a place for everyone
at the table of Christ.
But does it have to be this table?
Do we have to kneel so close
that I am aware
of only those who have hurt me?
I don't want to share the Body of Christ
with those who do not value me.

But does it have to be this table
at which I am offered Christ,
who gives peace and New Life,
which I cannot believe will flow

into a heart as cold as stone?

But is that my fault,
for not loving and forgiving,
for speaking empty words
of peace and trust?
Can God's mercy flow
through an unwilling heart?

And who is forgiving whom?
The betrayed forgiving the betrayer for losing faith?
The faithful forgiving the deserters?
The betrayer forgiving themselves for harming?
The denier forgiving themselves for weakness?
The grieving forgiving God for bereaving?
God forgiving us all for frailty.

And that is where God trips me up.
If we exclude one sinner from one table,
where do we stop?
The table of God is for everyone
or it is for no one
Or we limit God
by our own prejudice
and inhibition.

If not at *this* table,
where will we find peace?
Where find the place from which to move on

from the fragility of survival,
and the acknowledgement of guilt?
If it is not at this table, together,
then we hinder God's love.

Details of the Illustrations

Where a title is underlined, this is the title given to the artwork that has been photographed. Copyright is only claimed here for the photograph. The copyright for the original artwork remains that of its creator and in all cases permission has been applied for.

Where only a title is given, the photographs were staged by the author and her 'angels' to illustrate this project or are photographs of props used for Holy Week worship. Those who kindly agreed to model for various poses are not named, however I should like to acknowledge that they are all 'angels' who have walked with me through struggles and thank them for their willing cooperation in my artistic endeavours.

(page numbers refer to the largest version of the illustration dates refer to the copyright date of each photograph)

Cover   *Ganagobie Cross,* Ganagobie Monastery, overlooking the Durance valley in Provence. (August 2003)

Dedication   *Friendship Statue,* soapstone statue hand carved and sold through the Fair Trade foundation. (January 2006)

p9   *Lower Borrowdale from Surprise View*, produced to illustrate the Road to Emmaus, but not used. (May 2012)

p11   *The Thinker*, sculpture by Helen Sinclair, displayed at the Himalayan Gardens, Grewelthorpe, North Yorks. The sculpture is set in a stream, as if life is washing over and around him whilst he ponders its meaning. (October 2017)

p13   *Love-Scarred Hands.* (See details for p191)

p14   *Rood Cross,* Clifton Parish Church, York. (July 2007)

p18   *The Abandoned Quarry on Iona.* (March 2013)

p19   *Brigid's Cross*, Grasmere Rush-bearing festival. (July 2017)

p24   *Olive Tree,* temperate biome, Eden Project, Cornwall. (August 2007)

INDEX OF BIBLICAL REFERENCES